More Praise for Visible Learners

"*Visible Learners* is the most comprehensive approach to the values of documentation and how to go about it yet published. This volume makes clear that documentation can serve a wide range of important purposes for learners and their teachers, their families, and even their larger communities. The authors' discussion of the positive uses of documentation in connection with formal state standards is not only very timely, but also very helpful and practical. This book should be available to all teachers of all ages and subjects, not only during their training, but also throughout their work with our children."
—**Lilian G. Katz, Ph.D.,** Professor Emerita & Clearinghouse on Early Education and Parenting, University of Illinois

"This smart book begins with a series of stories about reciprocal learning by young people at different levels of schooling. Next it proposes that readers analyze those stories in terms of multiple insights gained from documentation, which can make learning, whether by individuals or groups, visible, and can indicate how that learning can be further sustained. The authors then face head-on the questions now so frequently asked about how documentation can support standard-based practice. Leaving no stone unturned, the authors construct on the basis of their extensive experience, a practical guide to structures, strategies, and tools for fostering learning in groups through documentation. Where the authors suggest that readers refer to the earlier book they produced together with Reggio Children, *Making Learning Visible,* I instead would insist that readers regard it as fundamental for understanding the principles that underlie this generous new work."
—**Lella Gandini,** U.S. Liaison for the Dissemination of the Reggio Emilia Approach

"With the challenge of preparing all students for college and career readiness and Common Core State Standards, there is agreement on this: students need to be independent, reflective learners, critical thinkers and problem solvers. How do we develop these attributes in students? *Visible Learners* offers a powerful answer: classrooms dedicated to the process of looking closely at student ideas—observing, documenting and analyzing to improve the quality of student work and understanding."
—**Ron Berger,** Chief Program Officer, Expeditionary Learning

For Andrew, Liz, Steve, and Terri for their support

Visible Learners

Promoting Reggio-Inspired Approaches in All Schools

Mara Krechevsky
Ben Mardell
Melissa Rivard
Daniel G. Wilson

Project Zero, Harvard Graduate School of Education

Foreword by Deborah Meier

JB JOSSEY-BASS™
A Wiley Brand

Cover design by Michael Cook
Cover image: Copyright © 2013 by Melissa Rivard

Published by Jossey-Bass
A Wiley Brand
One Montgomery Street, Suite 1200, San Francisco, CA 94104-4594—www.josseybass.com

The names of the teachers and many of the students have not been changed, though in a few cases pseudonyms are used for students.

Jossey-Bass books and products are available through most bookstores. To contact Jossey-Bass directly call our Customer Care Department within the U.S. at 800-956-7739, outside the U.S. at 317-572-3986, or fax 317-572-4002.

Wiley also publishes its books in a variety of electronic formats and by print-on-demand. Some material included with standard print versions of this book may not be included in e-books or in print-on-demand. If the version of this book that you purchased references media such as a CD or DVD that was not included in your purchase, you may download this material at http://booksupport.wiley.com. For more information about Wiley products, visit www.wiley.com.

Library of Congress Cataloging-in-Publication Data

Krechevsky, Mara.
    Visible learners : promoting Reggio-inspired approaches in all schools / Mara Krechevsky, Ben Mardell, Melissa Rivard, Daniel G. Wilson.
        pages cm
    Includes bibliographical references and index.
    ISBN 978-1-118-34569-6 (pbk.), ISBN 978-1-118-42032-4 (pdf), ISBN 978-1-118-41692-1 (epub), ISBN 978-1-118-67038-5 (mobipocket)
    1. Group work in education.   2. Reggio Emilia approach (Early childhood education)
I. Mardell, Ben.   II. Rivard, Melissa, 1964–   III. Wilson, Daniel G., 1969–   IV. Title.
    LB1032.K68 2013
    372.21–dc23
                            2013006255

Printed in the United States of America
FIRST EDITION
PB Printing   10 9 8 7 6 5 4 3 2 1

Contents

Acknowledgments

In keeping with this book's focus on individual and group learning, our work has been inspired and sustained by the contributions of numerous colleagues and organizations. We would like to thank the Atlantic Philanthropies, the Massachusetts Department of Elementary and Secondary Education, and the Barr Foundation for their support in funding Project Zero and pre-K–12 teachers and teacher educators in the Boston area. In particular, we are grateful to Angela Covert and Kim Haskins for their vision and commitment to this work. We would also like to thank the Ohio Department of Education for its support of the Making Learning Visible (MLV) work at the Wickliffe Progressive Community School in Upper Arlington, Ohio.

An enormous amount of gratitude goes to the teachers, administrators, and high school students who participated in the MLV seminars: Aaron Levy, Adeleine Rodene, Amanda Van Vleck, Annie Sevelius, Ariela Rothstein, Betsy Damian, Bobbi Rosenquest, Cathy Milne, Char Skidmore, Cheryl Sutter, Chris Bucco, Chris Low, Cindy Snow, Clancie Wilson, Dan Monahan, Danikka Giarratani, David Ramsey, Deb Dempsey, Debi Milligan, Doug Anderson, Ellen Goldberg, Frances Farrell, Gene Thompson-Grove, Gerardo Martinez, Gina Stefanini, Gizelle Dizon, Graciela Hopkins, Heather Moore Wood, Heather Nord, Heidi Lyne, Ian Hamel, Jennifer Hogue, Jill Berg, Joan Soble, Joanne Cleary, Johanna Grochowalski, Jon Hirst, Karen Daniels, Kendra McLaughlin, Kerrie-Lee Walker, Kevin Depin, Kyle Dodson, Lesley Strang, Lin Tucker, Lindy Johnson, Lisa Dittrich, Lisa Fiore, Lori Rivera, Lynn Hurley, Lynn Stuart, Maggie Donovan, Marc Kenen, Maren Oberman, Marguerite Hicks, Marina Boni, Masami Stampf, Melissa Tonachel, Molander Etienne, Nicole Chasse, Pam Richardson, Phyllis Bretholtz, Rachel Hayashi, Rachelle Milord, Rawchayl Sahadeo, Sarae Pacetta, Sarah Fiarman, Sarah Mayper, Sevan Marinilli, Stephanie Cox Suarez, Tassia Thomas, Tavia Mead, Tina Blythe, Todd Curtis, Una MacDowell, Yvonne Young, and Zoe Cohen. We are honored to be your colleagues and deeply grateful for your dedication to exploring new possibilities for teaching and learning. Each of you contributed enormously to our understanding of how to put these ideas into practice in US schools across the grades. Without you, there would be no book.

We also want to thank the administrators and colleagues of our MLV seminar members who provided support and participated in MLV work at the school level: the entire staff and parents at the Baldwin Early Learning Center in Brighton, Massachusetts; Jennifer Van Hill, Marlon Davis, Sherley Bretous-Carré, and Suzannah Bukenya at the Benjamin Banneker Public Charter School in Cambridge, Massachusetts; Chris Saheed, Damon Smith, Doug McGlathery, and all of the members of the exhibition group over the years at Cambridge Rindge and Latin School; Andrea Doane, Beth Williams, Bethany Bergeron, Bonnie Michal, Erin McKenna, Liz Gelotte, and MaryBeth Zabowsky at the Devotion School in Brookline, Massachusetts; and Amber McKinnon, Erin Daly, Genteen Lacet Jean-Michel, Julie Walsh, Kirstin Peth, Marie Mullen, Melissa Provencial, and Radha Hernandez at the Lee Academy Pilot School in Boston.

Additionally, we want to acknowledge the teachers and others who collected documentation for and contributed significantly to the writing of the learning portraits that ground the ideas discussed in this book: Nicole Chasse and Lissett Babaian; Mandy Locke and Matt Leaf; Joan Soble; Doug McGlathery, Joan Brunetta, and Nora Sears; Susan Durkee; and Amanda Van Vleck.

We extend our gratitude to Chris Collaros, Debi Binkley, Fred Burton, Jeannie Sperling, Maureen Reedy, and Sabrina Walters of the Wickliffe Progressive Community School for inviting us to work with the extraordinary staff and families of the Wickliffe learning community. We treasure the many professional and personal relationships we have formed over the years; we have learned a tremendous amount from all of you.

Over the years we have had the pleasure of working with a number of talented researchers and graduate students who made critical contributions to the MLV project. We extend our thanks to Andrea Thies, Arzu Mistry, Beau Martin, Carolyn DeCristofano, Casey Presby, Celina Benevides, Elena Belle White, Ian Parker-Renga, Janet Stork, John Spudich, Lissett Babaian, Matthew Cannavale, Sara Hendren, Susanna Lara, and Terri Turner.

A number of critical friends have supported us in developing the ideas presented in this book. Among this group are Aliyah Mahmoud, Jeanne Bamberger, Lella Gandini, Peggy Kemp, Ron Berger, Ron Ritchhart, and Sarah Fiarman.

Our thanks to Howard Gardner, Steve Seidel, Tavia Mead, Liz Merrill, and Joan Soble for providing helpful feedback to drafts of this book. Special thanks to Tina Blythe for her careful and astute reading of a preliminary version of the book.

We appreciate the support of the Jossey-Bass team—Kate Bradford, Justin Frahm, Susan Geraghty, and Nana Twumasi—for their receptivity to publishing a book that would speak to a spectrum of pre-K–12 educators via a set of "learning portraits," more traditional chapters, and practical tools.

This book would not be possible without the support and inspiration of our colleagues at two organizations. Project Zero has served as our intellectual home and we are grateful for the rich learning environment it provides. Howard Gardner has given generously of his time and counsel throughout this work. We are especially appreciative of the Dumbledore of Making Learning Visible, Steve Seidel, who guided and enriched this work every step of the way with his wisdom, his wit, and his humanity.

We are also grateful to our colleagues at the Municipal Infant-Toddler Centers and Preschools of Reggio Emilia, Italy, and their sister organization, Reggio Children. Many of the ideas and practices in this book were developed or inspired by these extraordinary centers and schools. Thank you to Paola Barchi, Angela Barozzi, Paola Cagliari, Marina Castagnetti, Francesca Davoli, Tiziana Filippini, Amelia Gambetti, Claudia Giudici, Francesca Marastoni, Isabella Meninno, Annamaria Mucchi, Giovanni Piazza, Evelina

Reverberi, Paola Ricco, Carla Rinaldi, Laura Rubizzi, Paula Strozzi, Vea Vecchi, and Emanuela Vercalli. They, along with dozens of other passionate educators, continue to create inspirational environments in which learners young and old can reach their full potential. A special grazie to Carlina Rinaldi and Tiziana Filippini, whose intellectual and personal support have sustained us over the years and across the ocean.

Finally, we thank the learners and their families for allowing us to use their stories and on whose behalf all of this work was conducted.

Foreword

I have never liked the word *accountability* when talking about our responsibilities as teachers and parents for our children. There is something about the word that leads us down the wrong path. What a pleasure, then, to watch how the authors of this book tackle the unprecedented focus on high-stakes testing as a response to accountability. They offer an alternative.

Years ago, my friend and colleague Edward (Ted) Chittenden reminded us that test scores were indirect evidence of something we had direct access to—the students and their work. There are lots of ways of showing what is happening in schools. This book helps us think about them all—and highlights the trade-offs that are always involved.

That is what this wonderful book is all about: using our powers of observation and discretion to make sense of what it is students are engaged in and whether we are moving in the right direction, need to reexamine our assumptions, or need to dig deeper to better make sense of what these young people are showing us. It is in this latter form that *Visible Learners* serves simultaneously as professional development and accountability to others.

It is rare these days to find a book that actually describes a classroom in which a teacher and students engage in learning together. As David Hawkins once put it—learning is a triangle with teacher and student at two corners and their common subject of study at the third. We adults join our students in uncovering puzzles of the mind, built around dilemmas presented by the world around us. When taken by themselves, the six learning portraits described in the first part of this book are a remarkable account of what real "project learning" is all about. It's not "word problems" but living complexities that fascinate. Equally critical to documenting these classroom projects is the authors' focus on "learning together"—within a classroom and a schoolhouse. Documentation of learning and of our teaching practice builds a richer collaborative learning setting not only for young people but also for adults. Seeing the same practices through the eyes of others is an essential part of strong professional development and the one most seriously lacking from our schools.

Each learning portrait presents its own challenges. The learning portrait "Grappling with Greatness" is an example of what Ted Sizer called "an essential question"—and this class's exploration of the idea is masterly, a reminder of what patient listening can uncover. In this portrait we see not only the children expanding but also their teacher. What I enjoyed was

Joan Soble's recognizing how often as teachers we seek agreement versus disagreement—as though all differences need to be resolved happily. She encouraged her students to argue with each other and defend their view, but they seemed too easily prepared to surrender and fall back on "difference" as a way to avoid reconsidering their own viewpoint and coming to consensus. However, in pushing this important idea she also began to see that "consensus not only might not be possible, but might be less important than she imagined."

Parts 1 and 2 build on this synergy between students and teacher. And in the final chapter in part 2 we complete the circle by exploring how such work can engage families—so often the missing link in young people's learning in school. Part 3 offers some wonderful tools for schools and teachers to use in examining these portraits, principles, and practices: how-tos for translating these ideas into practice in actual classrooms. The authors have culled some of the best I've seen.

The approaches to documentation and group learning that the authors describe to help us adults make better sense of our work and our students are similar to the Descriptive Review processes developed by Pat Carini at the Prospect School and Center for Education and Research in North Bennington, Vermont. Each approach has distinctive elements but it is reassuring to see how well they fit together. Each approach stimulates us to attend to the ways in which we can broaden our viewpoint about young people and their work by sharing perspectives that lead not to arguments so much as a widening of possibilities.

I have enjoyed following the Reggio Emilia work but am sometimes put off by the amount of documentation involved. In *Visible Learners* I came to understand how documentation serves many different purposes, all focused on making the student and his or her learning more visible. It is this visibility that enables parents and teachers, teachers and students, and teachers and other colleagues to join together better in making the world more visible to the student. We can see with our eyes and be blind to what is in front of us far too easily in most classrooms. But the careful and shared documentation that is described on these pages makes it harder to maintain the view that such documentation is a luxury—a time-consuming form of public relations. In fact, such documentation can, in the long run, be a time-saver when learner and teacher get a clearer picture of what is going on.

What is special about this book is that it describes, as Lev Vygotsky notes, how "children grow into the intellectual life of those around them"[1]. . . if such a life exists! How rarely do we remember that we can only "pass on" to young people what we ourselves understand, care about, and value. It is through our enactment of such values that young people learn to value them, too.

I remembered years of struggling with the balance between losing myself in engagement with my students and more distant observation. We teachers sometimes feel a conscientious need to earn our pay by "doing" something, being "hands on"—telling, explaining, and giving feedback. But sitting back and observing, sometimes with clear intent and sometimes without, I'm reminded, is a hard and critical part of our professional duty. In part because I enjoyed adult company I also soon discovered what the authors remind us of here—that the adults in schools are in the process of learning, too, and time must be made for them to learn from and with each other.

I learned the hard way. I hope that readers of this book, whether experienced or inexperienced, will be able to step back more often and more wisely than I did because of these accounts, stories, and tools.

Deborah Meier
Founder of Central Park East Schools, New York City
and Mission Hill Pilot School, Boston

Introduction

Loris Malaguzzi, the founder of the Reggio Emilia schools, once said, "Learning and teaching should not stand on opposite banks and just watch the river flow by; instead, they should embark together on a journey down the water."[1] This book is about the journey down the water. It is about the marriage of listening and intentionality. It is about how documentation of individual and group learning strengthens and enriches the dialogue between teaching and learning inside and outside of classrooms and schools.

Globalization and the new economy of the twenty-first century demand the ability to learn and function as part of increasingly diverse groups. In an interconnected and rapidly changing world, our knowledge of ourselves as individual and group learners becomes more important. Yet the acquisition of knowledge is still primarily viewed as an individual process. Thinking and learning are generally considered individual rather than social or communicative acts. Virtually all assessment and many aspects of instruction still focus on promoting individual performance and achievement. In this book, we examine how the combined practices of group learning and documentation of learning processes and products lead to powerful teaching and learning for students, teachers, and the larger community.

This is not a typical how-to book. It is purposefully designed to bridge teaching levels and subject matter—from preschool to high school, from art to algebra. We also seek to reach administrators looking for ways to create stimulating and memorable learning environments for students, teachers, and families. Our goal is to inspire and enable educators to build a classroom and school culture that makes powerful learning moments more likely to occur—for their students, for themselves, and for the community at large. Though our intent is to provoke contemplation of the possible, we ground the ideas and practices we put forth in research.

Inspired by the work in Reggio Emilia as well as research-based practices developed at Project Zero, the concepts and practices described in this book grew out of years of close collaboration with US teachers. For more than a decade, the authors of this book have collaborated with more than one hundred US teachers, predominantly in urban public schools, to investigate questions such as, How do observing and documenting learning change the nature of that learning? What is the relationship between individual and group learning? When does a group become a learning group? The enormous dedication, contributions, and insights of these teachers are reflected in this book.

History

In 1997, educators from the Municipal Preschools and Infant-Toddler Centers of Reggio Emilia (a small city in northern Italy) and Project Zero (a research organization at the Harvard Graduate School of Education) came together to investigate the group as a learning environment and documentation as a way to make visible and shape how and what we learn. Since the late 1960s, Project Zero researchers have studied the development of learning processes in children, adults, and organizations. The Reggio preschools originated from the efforts of parents in local communities to rebuild their schools after the devastation of World War II. For more than forty-five years, educators in this exceptional set of thirty-four municipal preschools and infant-toddler centers have carefully researched, documented, and facilitated children's learning, bringing international attention to children's capacities as individual and group learners.

Most of the research in this early phase of our work was grounded in the Reggio classrooms. In 2001, we published a framework for understanding, documenting, and supporting individual and group learning in the book *Making Learning Visible: Children as Individual and Group Learners*, coauthored by Project Zero researchers and Reggio educators. *Making Learning Visible* included a number of visual essays—mini-stories in prose and images—of children in Reggio classrooms learning, playing, and working together. In one mini-story, three five-year-old girls worked for an hour drawing a beautiful and detailed map of their city (see figure 1). In another, four- and five-year-olds illustrated

Figure 1. City of Reggio Emilia Drawn by Five-Year-Old Girls

instructions for ring-around-the-rosy to be shared with younger children. A third story describes how a group of five- and six-year-olds developed a complex theory of how fax machines work.

The benefits of children participating in such rich and multifaceted learning experiences are immense. For those unfamiliar with Reggio, *Making Learning Visible* raised the question of whether children elsewhere, in different types of schools, could participate in similar types of experiences and whether these strategies might support the learning of older students as well. As one middle school teacher commented, "If four-year-olds can do this, imagine what fourteen-year-olds might do."

Since the publication of *Making Learning Visible*, we have worked with US teachers, primarily in Massachusetts and Upper Arlington, Ohio, to document children's learning through notes, photographs, video, transcripts, and student work. We have collected, shared, analyzed, and interpreted this documentation in small groups and large groups, with children and adults, in seminars and on-the-fly. This book shares the results of our research.

The Goals of This Book

Visible Learners has three main goals. First, we want to challenge readers' thinking about what is possible for children of any age by sharing rich examples of visible learning in a variety of subject matters and age levels. Traditionally, the Reggio approach has been associated with early childhood; to the best of our knowledge, its potential for inspiring and enriching teaching and learning for older students has yet to be fully explored. The six learning portraits in part 1 describe in images and prose different possibilities for visible learning across grades and subject matter. The portraits can be used by groups of teachers to support, challenge, or extend their thinking about powerful opportunities for learning. They can also be used with students to talk about what happens when groups come together to learn. Teacher educators can use the learning portraits as provocations for developing compelling curriculum or as illustrations of theory in action.

Our second goal is to describe the underlying pedagogical principles and practices at work in making learning visible so that teachers, teacher leaders, administrators, teacher educators, and professional development providers can reflect on and adapt these ideas for different contexts. The chapters in part 2 draw heavily on the six learning portraits to illustrate the principles and practices. We also situate the work in the current context of unprecedented focus on high-stakes testing and accountability. We show how standards can work together with practices of group learning and documentation, and propose an alternative way to think about accountability.

In chapter 7, "Making Learning and Learners Visible," we make the case that learning should be a visible activity that develops students' intellectual capacities as well as their individual and group identities as learners. We identify five key principles or dimensions of visible learning—purposeful, social, representational, empowering, and emotional—and illustrate each dimension with examples from the learning portraits.

In chapter 8, "Unpacking the Practice of Group Learning," we describe why learning in groups, particularly small groups, is an essential component of any powerful learning environment. We identify five strategies that promote learning in groups—nurturing children's capacities to learn together, designing engaging tasks that benefit from a group perspective, facilitating conversations that deepen learning, forming groups intentionally, and choreographing individual, small-group, and whole-class learning.

In chapter 9, "Unpacking the Practice of Documentation," we examine the concept and practices of documentation. We describe how documentation serves different learning purposes and audiences across four contexts—inside and outside the classroom and during and after a learning experience. We then outline four practices of documentation—observing, recording, interpreting, and sharing—and suggest strategies within each that teachers can use to support learning and make it visible.

Carrying out this work amid pressures of coverage, testing, and standards is an ongoing challenge. In chapter 10, "Making Learning Visible in an Age of Accountability," we draw on the learning portraits to show how making learning and learners visible can help teachers address standards and reframe notions of accountability. Making learning visible helps teachers build bridges between standards and their students, create shared reference points for what standards look like in practice, and demonstrate valued forms of learning not often reflected on standardized tests. We conclude by suggesting that accountability can be thought of as responsibility to oneself, to each other, and to the larger community.

Our third goal is to provide a set of tools that teachers can use or adapt to make learning and learners visible in their classrooms and schools. Presented in a primarily one- to two-page format, the tools in part 3 identify specific steps for implementing group learning and documentation strategies. Preservice teachers can experiment with the tools in their practicums as they learn the craft of teaching, whereas in-service teachers can use them to support their inquiry or as part of professional development initiatives. The tools are grouped into five categories:

> In chapter 11, "Supporting Learning in Groups in the Classroom," we include tools for creating and sustaining learning groups and fostering a culture of dialogue in the classroom.

> In chapter 12, "Supporting Learning in Groups in the Staffroom," we share activities, structures, and conversation protocols for supporting adult learning groups.

> In chapter 13, "Documenting Individual and Group Learning," we provide resources for adults (and students) to understand, create, and share documentation, including technical considerations and guidelines for choosing a documentation tool.

> In chapter 14, "Engaging Families in Supporting Student Learning," we suggest ways to inform families about and involve them in MLV ideas and support their child's learning at home and in school.

> In chapter 15, "Making Learning Visible beyond the Classroom," we offer tools and templates for making learning and learners visible outside of classrooms and schools.

We invite readers to move around in the book, though we recommend reading part 1 before part 2 because the classroom illustrations in part 1 ground many of the ideas and principles shared in part 2. Some readers may prefer to focus only on the tools in part 3 or to concentrate on the chapters that address either documentation or group learning in particular. Whatever path you take, we hope the passage will be as generative as the destination.

In talking about the balance between teaching and learning, Loris Malaguzzi said, "It is obvious that between learning and teaching, we honor the first. It is not that we ostracize teaching, but we tell it, 'Stand aside for a while and leave room for learning, observe carefully what children do, and then, if you have understood well, perhaps teaching will be different from before.'"[2] The twin practices described in this book—documentation and learning from and with others—are one way to bring together teaching and learning in their journey down the water.

PART I: Six Learning Portraits

Chapters 1 through 6 depict six learning portraits from kindergarten through twelfth grades in several disciplines. It is not necessary to read through the portraits sequentially before moving onto other portions of the book; rather, feel free to read those portraits that speak to your interests. If, later in the book, you come across a reference to a portrait that is unfamiliar to you, we encourage you to return to that chapter and read the portrait.

As you read the portraits, we invite you to consider the following questions:

- In what ways do you see learners and learning being made visible?
- How do the practices of group learning and documentation support each other?
- What roles do the teachers and students play in supporting their own and each other's learning?
- How do the practices in these classrooms reflect or extend the ways you make learning visible in your classroom?

Chapter 1
The Yellow Door
Turning Problems into Projects in Kindergarten

Teachers
Nicole Chasse and John Walker

Children
Amelia, Ava, Betel, Durjoy,
Hakim, Sajan, Tamar, and William

This learning portrait describes how two teachers use student conflict in a play area of their kindergarten classroom to promote children's collaborative inquiry, social and artistic development, and mathematical reasoning.

Children in Nicole Chasse's kindergarten class at the Edward Devotion School* liked to build in the block area. They built and rebuilt sturdy ramps for trucks to speed down and homes for the wooden animals. The only problem was that everyone liked to use the yellow door. As one child named Durjoy explained, **"The yellow door was better than the red windows because it was tall enough for the black horse to walk through. But we only had one door and people were having trouble sharing."** Consequently, the yellow door led to lots of arguments.

---

*The Edward Devotion School is the largest pre-K–8 elementary school in Brookline, Massachusetts. The Devotion School serves more than seven hundred students, with a large population of English language learners and students who require intensive social and emotional supports.

Growing tired of children's increasing arguments over the door, one morning Nicole asked Hakim, Durjoy, and Sajan, **"Do you think the block area would be more fun without the door, because it seems like the door is causing too many problems for you to enjoy yourselves?"**

Unhappy with the prospect of losing the door, the boys were motivated to find another way to solve the problem.

"Buy more doors!" one boy shouted. Nicole explained that this idea would require money they did not have and encouraged them to keep thinking.

"Make more doors!"

Nicole was intrigued by this idea. She could imagine many opportunities for learning as well as challenges that she posed to the boys: **"How could we make doors just as good as the yellow door so people would use them?"** Hakim, Durjoy, and Sajan suggested asking John Walker, the assistant teacher, to help because he was an expert woodworker and the yellow door was made out of wood. Later that day, the three boys presented the idea to John and the rest of the class. The idea was received enthusiastically and the door project was born.

The Planning Phase

All the other wood projects we did, John Walker thought up. But this project, we actually worked on the beginning plans.—Amelia

The children's desire to make a door exactly like the cherished yellow door offered many opportunities to advance the children's learning and make connections across several strands of the kindergarten curriculum—including arts, English language arts, and math. Because the children had already done some observational drawing, John suggested interested students make sketches or "plans" for the doors based on careful observation of the yellow door, which he could then use to make the door "kits." The children would then help with the finishing—sanding, choosing colors, and painting.

Eight children volunteered to make plans. Some students sketched freestyle, whereas others such as Tamar chose to be more precise by measuring the original door with a ruler to find its exact dimensions. Tamar's idea inspired others to use the ruler so John explained the concepts of length and width. They discovered the door was exactly 5½ × 4 inches.

The "Door Hunt": Collecting Data on Doors

While waiting for John to build the door kits, Nicole took advantage of children's increased interest in doors and asked if anyone wanted to explore the school to see what other kinds of doors they could find. The children loved the idea. Not only did it tap into their fascination with doors but also, as Ava later said, they were able to **"go to places that kindergartners don't [usually] get to go to."** Nicole suggested children count and record the different types of doors they saw but did not provide specific instructions on how to record.

Each child took a clipboard, paper, and pencil to record the information. Nicole and John alternated accompanying the small groups, taking pictures or video to document the different doors and children's observations along the way.

The children's notations reflected the different features they noticed about doors as well as the different methods they each invented to record the data.

Some children recorded the order in which they encountered specific doors, others recorded the number of doors they found with particular features, and still others recorded observations in writing. Sajan recorded the doors he found by writing pairs of contrasting features, **"Red and not red, two [doors] and one [door], things [on the door] and no things [on the door]."**

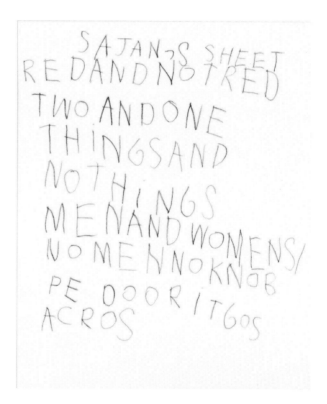

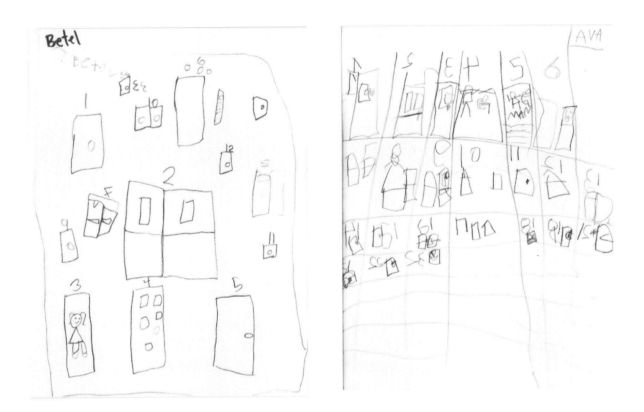

In one group, Amelia (who dubbed this part of the project **"the door hunt"**) organized her paper into a graph to make room for all the doors she found. When children shared the data they collected with the whole group, the other children found Amelia's method very appealing. The next day, another group followed suit and created similar grid patterns on their paper.

Organizing and Sharing the Data

When Nicole and John looked at the children's data, they noticed the children naturally gravitated toward identifying the doors' different attributes. Because counting, describing, and comparing measurable attributes and classifying objects are important parts of the kindergarten math curriculum, they approached Ms. Boss, the school's math specialist, to seek help on planning next steps that would continue to deepen these skills. The next day, Nicole, John, and Ms. Boss presented the class with a new provocation: **"Can you choose one attribute and collect a new set of door information based on only that one attribute?"**

Ms. Boss gave the students a blank piece of paper, demonstrated how to draw a graph, and reviewed the question she had posed—discussing the meaning of "attribute" by using examples from the data the children had collected (size, color, material, unique features, etc.). Before setting off with clipboards and graph paper, each child chose an attribute on which to record information. Tamar, Sajan, Ava, and Amelia all decided to record color; Ethan W. chose size.

After the children collected their data on color and size, Nicole took them to the fourth grade hallway to look at the fourth-graders' graphs of "leaf fall data." She pointed out how they could clearly see which trees lost the most or least leaves in certain weeks. The kindergartners noticed that the fourth-graders used labels and organized the graphs around the types of trees, the weeks they were observing, and the number of fallen leaves. Nicole proposed a new challenge: **"Could we take the information we collected from our door graphs and make it into a graph that others in the school could read?"**

The group was up for the challenge. Nicole worked with small groups in the hallway while John helped out with the rest of the class. Nicole gave the first group of five a choice of working alone or with a partner and a choice of paper—large lined chart paper or blank white drawing paper. Sajan and Tamar decided to merge their data into one graph. Betel, who had opted out of the door hunts, worked with Ava to transfer her data into a graph on the chart paper. Durjoy decided to work on his own. Here we follow Ava and Betel as they work.

Ava, who seemed to understand the concept of graphing and what it was for, first explained to Betel, **"It's lines going that way (indicating horizontally across the page) and lines going down with things in the middle. If we just had a blank piece of paper, it wouldn't be really organized."** Then Ava shared her strategy: **"I'm writing down from this (indicating her data collection sheet which she organized by color)—purple, green, black, and peach"** (pointing to the top of the larger sheet where she has written the colors). Nicole asked Ava what she planned to do with the markers. Ava responded, looking as much at Betel as Nicole to be sure Betel was clear about the plan, **"We're going to draw how many doors there are here (indicating the data sheet) over here (indicating the graph)."** Satisfied that the pair had a plan for moving their graph forward, Nicole went to help Sajan and Tamar—who were still confused—get started.

The hallway began to fill with animated discussions within and across groups. Sajan and Tamar created a counting game and pretended to count all the way up to one hundred. Durjoy ran up with great urgency, **"Does . . . is *big* . . . b . . . b-i-g?"** Sajan confirmed and Durjoy ran back to share the answer with Amelia. Meanwhile, Ava and Betel were engaged in deep negotiation about their shared task.

After filling in the column on the graph representing the number of purple doors, Ava said to Betel, who was holding a green marker, **"Color in three spaces. Okay?"**

Betel disagreed. **"No. I want to color over here."** Betel had yet to grasp the purpose behind their coloring. She seemed to base her decision of where to color on other criteria. Ava took a different tack, **"I mean, color in three spaces in this green line. Okay?"**

Betel seemed convinced by this and started coloring in the spaces indicated by Ava.

Ava, perhaps recognizing that Betel had just made a compromise, offered her friend a compliment, **"Wow. You're a better colorer than me, Betel."** After carefully coloring in one green square, Betel stopped and put the cap back on the green marker, indicating her completion of the task. Ava said in an encouraging tone, **"So now you can do two more. Okay?"**

Betel responded somewhat enigmatically, **"This is one door (pointing to the green door she has just colored) and now we have to do three more."** Without looking, Betel picked up a new marker and started coloring in the box immediately below the green one. Ava quickly tried another approach, **"I've got an idea, Betel!"** Grabbing her data sheet and showing it to Betel, Ava said, **"Don't count the purple because we already did the purple. Follow this green one. You just have to do two more in this green line."** Still not grasping the concept, Betel said good-naturedly, **"But, I can do red?"** Ava, after looking around for Nicole, who had gone back into the classroom, seemed to give up on helping her friend understand the concepts underlying their work and resorted to a more directive approach. **"No. You need to do two more squares of green."** Betel accepted this without further question and followed Ava's direction. Ava supervised.

After Ava took a turn coloring in two black squares for the two doors she recorded on her hunt, Betel announced that she would do blue. Ava explained, **"Well, you can't do blue because I don't have blue on my graph."**

Betel's eyes widened as she seemed to grasp the concept behind what they were doing, **"Oh! Because there were no blue doors?"** Great excitement ensued once the two girls were "on the same page." Together, they went through the chart again, with Ava naming the colors and the corresponding numbers of doors and Betel exclaiming, **"Now, I see!"**

With one column remaining on the chart indicating one peach door, both girls reached for the orange marker—the closest color to peach in the basket. Without a word, they each grabbed an orange marker and filled in the last box together, whispering and laughing as they colored.

Later Nicole and John reviewed the completed graphs along with video documentation of the groups working together to see how well each child had understood the concept of collecting and transferring data onto a graph and what further instruction might be needed.

Finishing the Doors

John used the children's designs to make six wooden door kits with doors and frames, which were then sanded and painted by small groups of students. Although the process for choosing a color for the kit varied across groups, it was always democratic. Students working in pairs tended toward compromise, with each one picking a color for the door or frame, whereas larger groups held votes or played rock, paper, scissors.

The Legacy of the Door Project

A few years after the project, Nicole asked several students to reflect on their experience. The students seemed to recognize that there was something special about the door project that made it stand out from other school experiences. Betel liked the project because it enabled her to slow down and concentrate her learning on one topic. **"We didn't rush in it. We just took our time . . . usually you have to do all these other things, but this time we just went on to [new] things about doors."**

Whereas many students identified going around the school collecting data as their favorite part of the project, Durjoy's nomination was **"when everybody stopped fighting over this original door."** Nicole concurred, observing that the tenor of the class, which prior to the door project had been characterized by conflict and strife, had become more harmonious and collaborative overall.

The door project's benefits were multifaceted. The project achieved the students' immediate goal of adding more doors to the block area and provided a range of learning opportunities along the way that directly connected to kindergarten curriculum standards. In the arts, students worked on representing their ideas in two and three dimensions, learned to mix colors, and worked with a variety of materials. They developed their verbal and writing abilities while working with each other in small groups and presenting their ideas and data in classroom meetings. The children's desire for precision led them to learn about measuring and dimensions and opened the door (no pun intended) for Nicole to work toward other mathematical standards such as describing and comparing attributes, placing and counting objects in categories, and identifying and describing shapes.

But the impact was even greater. When these students graduated from kindergarten, they left behind the doors they had made for future kindergarten classes to enjoy—turning self-interested conflicts into a generous gift to others.

My sister is playing with the doors now.—Amelia

Chapter 2

The Vernal Pool
Seventh-Graders Investigate and Protect a Local Habitat

FAIRY SHRIMP
(EUBRANCHIPUS VERNALIS)

Teachers
Mandy Locke and Matt Leaf

Students
Seventh Grade Class of 2008

This learning portrait explains how an English teacher and science teacher facilitate a year-long interdisciplinary inquiry into a local natural habitat to advance the writing skills, scientific reasoning, and citizenship of their middle school students.

According to *Life in a Vernal Pool*, a guidebook created by Mandy Locke's and Matt Leaf's seventh grade science and ELA classes at the Four Rivers Charter Public School,* *Eubranchipus vernalis*, the common fairy shrimp (depicted in the water color painting above), "have translucent bodies that refract light," creating an appearance that alternates between yellow, green, blue, and red. The book explains that these diminutive creatures feed on

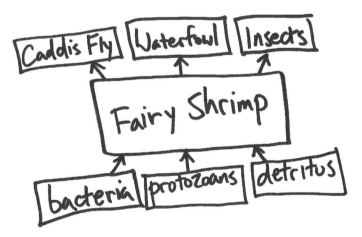

*Four Rivers Charter Public School is a grades 7–12 public school in Greenfield, Massachusetts (population 17,400). The school serves two hundred students of which 21 percent receive free or reduced lunch. Four Rivers is an Expeditionary Learning school featuring inquiry-based curriculum. For more information about Expeditionary Learning, visit http://elschools.org.

bacteria, protozoa, and the detritus of fallen leaves, and provide sustenance to an array of predators (see the food chain on the previous page). Because of their size and secretive nature, fairy shrimp are rarely seen, even by frequent visitors to New England forests.

The guidebook goes on to say that fairy shrimp is an "obligate specie" whose survival is dependent on vernal pools. These ephemeral bodies of water play a critical role in the eco-system of northern forests by providing essential breeding grounds for several species of frogs and salamanders (and fairy shrimp) to lay their eggs, safe from fish that inhabit lakes and ponds. The presence of fairy shrimp is a key criterion for certifying and protecting a body of water as a vernal pool.

The Vernal Pool Expedition

Five years prior, Mandy had attended a presentation by fellow Expeditionary Learning teachers from the King Middle School in Portland, Maine. Inspired by their work, she enlisted Matt in conducting an interdisciplinary project in which students spent the late winter and early spring creating a guide to some part of the natural world. Reflecting on that project, Mandy and Matt felt the students did strong work but worried that they did not make an emotional connection to the topic. Beyond being something to do in school, the project did not seem to matter to their students.

To begin a new project, Mandy and Matt gathered together their thirty-two students (the seventh grade at Four Rivers is split into two classes). Mandy and Matt knew that their students, in their first year at the seventh to twelfth grade school, were unfamiliar with "expeditions," so they had thought carefully about how to draw them into this collective, cross-disciplinary, real-world-based project. Mandy began, **"You have probably heard of the animal expedition. In the past, students have become experts about endangered species worldwide and in Massachusetts. Last year we created a CD about the wildlife in the Connecticut River Valley."**

Matt continued, **"This year we want to put your expertise to work. We want to focus on a particular place—the vernal pool that forms in Highland Park each spring. Even though there are several vernal pools in Greenfield, none are certified by the state. We want you to use your research to get this pool protected. We also want to make a guidebook that will interest people in vernal pools and that they can take into the woods and use."**

The four-month project included efforts to obtain state certification for the pool (requiring an in-depth data collection process) and the creation of a field guide involving individual, small-group, and whole-group work in an extensive drafting and feedback process. Or, in the students' words, **"bouncing ideas off friends," "friendly debates," "lots of revisions," "finding critters,"** and **"getting to be outside."**

Data Collection and Research: "What Is It?" and "How Can You Prove It?"

In all, the students made eight visits to the vernal pool. The first trip occurred when there was still snow on the ground so students could see where the pool's water came from. The group collected one cubic meter of snow to bring back to school to see how much liquid it produced.

Subsequent visits focused on learning more about the pool and its inhabitants and collecting the data necessary to have the pool certified. The Massachusetts Department of Fisheries and Wildlife produces a data checklist that names all the

information required for vernal pool certification. The checklist served as the official data collection sheet for the class. A master sheet was kept in the classroom and students brought copies of it on their visits.

As the seventh-graders explored the pool, often with the aid of dip nets, they made exciting discoveries. They came to Mandy and Matt to show them the eggs or salamanders they found, claiming they had discovered important data for the certification process. Faced with these claims, the teachers' refrain was always, **"How do you know?"** and **"How can you prove it?"**

Students used digital cameras to capture key discoveries and provide proof of their findings, both for classmates not on the visit and for the state agency. The question **"How do you know?"** was answered back in the classroom by researching, for example, whether the creature a student had found was a water boatman or a water strider.

The students visited the pool in two groups—one class in the morning and the other in the afternoon. This schedule allowed for two data counts each day to verify measurements taken and to ensure that the data collected were accurate and complete. The two-hour time difference between visits often resulted in a significant rise in temperature that altered the behavior of frogs and salamanders (cold-blooded amphibians become more active as external temperature rises).

In late April, the first group (who visited the pool earlier in the day) told the second group that there wasn't much activity. When the second class arrived at the pool, they heard a cacophony of wood frogs calling for mates. Mandy overheard two students hypothesize that the water temperature must have increased and noted this misconception. During the next visit, Mandy and Matt asked their students to measure the air and water temperature during both visits. The students' measurements revealed that, although air temperature can be quite variable, water temperature remains relatively stable throughout the day.

"Where Does the Energy Come From?"

Another misconception related to the energy sources for the pool. During another visit, Mandy overheard Laura, Garrett, Luz, and Amelia wondering, **"Why doesn't the pool fill up with leaves?"**

At their customary after-school debrief, Mandy shared this conversation with Matt. They wondered if students understood how leaves contribute to life in the pool and if the students' question might serve as an entry point into the concept of food webs (part of the seventh grade science standards).

Mandy brought the question to the whole class, asking, **"Because no water flows into the pool, where does the energy come from to support life?"** Students immediately responded, **"The sun."** Although the sun is the ultimate source of energy, Mandy wanted the students to understand the process by which frogs, salamanders, and other animal life access that energy (e.g., by eating plants that store energy from the sun, not by eating the sun directly). To help students better understand the workings of the pool, Mandy gave them a reading about food webs and chains. She then asked small groups to map the flow of energy on large sheets of paper, a process that each student repeated individually for the particular species they were studying for the guidebook.

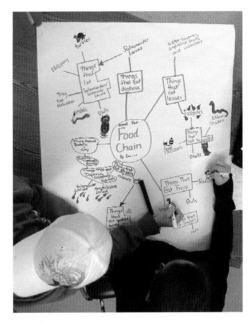

Creating the Field Guide

Including the glossary, *Life in a Vernal Pool: Field Guide and Folktales* is 156 pages long. There are folktales, scientific descriptions, and watercolor paintings of thirty-five species. But it is not the size of the book that is most impressive; rather, it is the detailed scientific information, the quality of the writing, and the beauty of the watercolor paintings that stand out.

Mandy and Matt structured the creation of each component of the book to foster collaboration that promoted individual and group learning. Writing physical descriptions of each animal began with the whole group reviewing various field guides. Most were deemed "boring" and lacking in voice (a major thrust of the seventh grade writing curriculum). However, students found the popular Stokes guides more engaging. Using these and work from previous years' guides as examples, the class constructed a rubric for physical description that included criteria for scientific content, vocabulary, sentence fluency, voice, organization, and conventions.

Despite this, many of the initial drafts were listings of traits—scientifically accurate but, well, boring. Matt set aside time at the end of each writing session for students to get feedback from peers. Based on the rubric they developed, classmates' suggestions included highlighting unusual or unexpected facts about the animal and using rhetorical questions to engage the reader.

As they read over their classmates' descriptions, the seventh-graders learned more about their species, discovering, for example, **"Hey, my animal eats your animal!"** Students used these discoveries to make their descriptions more specific (e.g., inserting *heron* for *bird*).

Multiple drafts resulted in descriptions with a stronger voice. The page on the air-breathing snail begins, "Have you ever seen a male snail or a female snail? I bet you haven't because there are no males or females. They are both!" The description of the blue spotted salamander includes a catchy introduction, "If you get your leg cut off, will it grow back? It will in the case of the blue spotted salamander," as well as information about its defense mechanism that students find particularly compelling—glands behind the tail that produce a noxious gas. The description of the fairy shrimp begins with a question:

> *Is it yellow, green, blue, or red? It's all of them. The fairy shrimp has a body that is translucent, which results in refraction or bending of surrounding light and colors. This creates an illusion of colors to appear on the fairy shrimp where it actually is not present.*

Creating watercolor paintings of the animals followed a similar process. In whole-group sessions students discussed how to produce different effects such as texture. Individual work time provided opportunities to get help from peers who were seen as painting experts (often not the same students considered to be expert writers). The final illustrations are both accurate and beautiful.

As production of the field guide neared completion, students organized committees to design the cover, write the glossary, and use a computer program to publish the book.

A Pool Protected

The students gathered an impressive array of data to support their case for protecting the pool. They identified and submitted the pool's exact location, along with topographical and assessor maps. They provided measurements (length, width, and maximum depth) along with a description of the pool's surroundings and data about the presence of obligate species. Photographs of the elusive fairy shrimp were the deciding evidence. A headline in the February 3, 2009, *Greenfield Recorder* reads "School Report Results in State Vernal Pool Designation." The article explains how efforts by Four Rivers' seventh-graders led the Commonwealth of Massachusetts to grant the vernal pool protection from development.

The field guide was donated to the local public library. It has been checked out fifteen times, including by a first grade teacher who uses the book to inspire her students to illustrate and draw local wildlife.

WOOD TURTLE
(CLEMMYS INSCULPTA)

AMERICAN TOAD
(BUFO AMERICANUS)

Recollections and Reflections

Four years after the publication of *Life in a Vernal Pool* six of the authors, now juniors, gather to talk about the expedition. They recalled their hard work on the book and the feeling of accomplishment when it was completed. They remembered the pride they felt in reading the newspaper article announcing the success of their efforts to gain state certification for the vernal pool (**"My mom made copies and sent it to the whole family."**) and their excitement in finding the fairy shrimp. The students were surprised they remembered so much about this curriculum.

All six students agreed they had never done anything like this before, either in scope or its group nature. (**"Before Four Rivers, school was sitting at your own desk doing your own work."**) Despite this lack of experience, they felt they were able to work together well because of the significance of the project (**"We were learning to do something to help our town."**) and because the work was active (**"not just reading from a textbook and sitting at a desk"**). They pointed to the guidebook as evidence that the project was a success.

Not that the project was easy. Several noted specific difficulties with painting and writing. But in the end, they **"were able to create a product that was far bigger than what we imagined in the beginning."**

Mandy and Matt's reflections mirrored those of their students. Mandy believed **"the magic of this project was working to get the pool certified."** She saw the seventh-graders move from "we are going to do field work" to "we are going to the vernal pool" to "we are going to our vernal pool." Mandy felt the vernal pool expedition was the right size for seventh-graders to investigate. In previous years the expedition had focused on larger environments such as the Connecticut River Valley. Narrowing the focus to the vernal pool **"got it just right."**

Matt recalled a moment in the project when, despite the enormity of the task, **"It stopped feeling like work. The students' excitement and their gains in writing, self-confidence, and getting along sustained me."** He was particularly proud that every seventh-grader contributed to the book. Even students with significant learning and emotional needs rose to the challenge. The group inspired them. Matt also noted that when these students took the state-mandated science and English tests in tenth grade, they scored the highest in the state.

Chapter 3
Grappling with Greatness
Negotiating Different Points of View in AP Literature

Teacher
Joan Soble

Students
Alex, Amalia, Jonah, Liam, Owen, Thalia, and Violet

This learning portrait details how an AP English teacher helps her eleventh- and twelfth-graders move beyond surface discussions about the nature of human greatness by engaging in and reflecting on their conversations in ways that complexify the topic and deepen everyone's learning.

Thalia: *I'm just a little confused because . . . I'm just like listening to everybody's points of view right now and, I don't know . . . I got that some of you think that greatness can't be achieved by everybody, and then Violet said that greatness can be achieved by like . . . someone who's . . . a normal guy, like a janitor. I'm just like trying to put everything together because it just doesn't make sense how . . . you guys don't think . . . everybody is born great . . .*

Violet: *Well, we all have different point of views.*

Thalia: *I should probably write [what I'm trying to say] down.*

Thalia and Violet, two students in Joan Soble's eleventh and twelfth grade Advanced Placement (AP) English literature and composition course at Cambridge Rindge and Latin School (CRLS),* were engaged with their classmates in a Socratic seminar about John Silber's *Of Mermaids and Magnificence.* The speech, delivered at the 1986 Boston University commencement, was intended to convey to students that greatness was within their reach. It assigns literature a crucial role

---

*Cambridge Rindge and Latin School (CRLS) is an urban high school in Cambridge, Massachusetts. CRLS serves more than 1,560 students, with 62 percent students of color, 28 percent English language learners, and 50 percent from low-income families.

in helping people respond with greatness to the challenges and opportunities life presents to them.

Joan first began thinking of human greatness as a good topic of study when reading *Team of Rivals: The Political Genius of Abraham Lincoln*. She saw this topic as critical for older high school students who, on the threshold of adulthood, were actively involved in envisioning their futures in a complex world in which greatness and celebrity can often be confused. Joan hoped that thinking deeply about greatness might help to shape their aspirations for themselves and their attitudes toward others.

Joan's AP students are a more diverse group than is typical for AP courses in most high schools. Because CRLS is an urban high school committed to empowering students who have historically been underrepresented in postsecondary education, administrators and teachers actively encourage such students to enroll in AP courses. So Joan considers her students in all their diversity as she looks for ways to engage them in this topic. For students coming from more privileged backgrounds (and who, research demonstrates, are likely to be headed for higher-paying, higher-status jobs in the future), she hopes that considering different types of greatness in works of literature can shape their choices about what to strive for and whom to help, champion, learn from, and even reward.

During the opening weeks of the semester, Joan worried that certain "less typical AP students"—such as Thalia, a Latina whose mother had not completed grammar school, and even Jonah who, though from a privileged background, viewed himself as a "good musician" rather than a "good student"—might become intimidated by students who were more confident about their verbal and intellectual abilities.

Joan videotaped a class to investigate her concerns and guide next steps. Reviewing the video confirmed Joan's worries. Violet seemed to understand the essay well, as evidenced by her confidently shared synopsis. However, Thalia, perhaps awed by the other students' comprehension, seemed to hesitate in expressing her opinion. When, at Joan's encouragement, she did, Joan felt that Violet was quick to label Thalia's comment as simply a different idea rather than explore its merit. Joan wondered if Thalia's desire to "write it down" reflected her sense that she had not been articulate enough to get others to think seriously about what she was saying. Thalia's ideas diverged from those of other students but resonated with Silber's assertion that we all have the potential for greatness. Thalia, like Joan, wanted her ideas to be considered rather than simply acknowledged. To Joan, the students seemed to be content with knowing each other's viewpoints but not willing to reconsider and possibly amend their initial ideas when encountering the ideas and viewpoints of their peers.

At the beginning of the course, Joan envisioned the class coming to a consensual understanding of the nature of human greatness. But now, Joan was beginning to wonder if shifts in understanding were possible. The students didn't seem to be listening closely enough to one another to understand how and why their views differed; "claiming difference" became a way to avoid reexamining individual thinking that was challenged. Furthermore, the students seemed to have no sense that they could strengthen their thinking, by either altering it or recommitting to it with greater perspective and conviction. Following this discussion, Amalia, one of the students, captured the elusiveness and potential usefulness of trying to reach consensus in one of her postings on Moodle, the school's online discussion forum.

October 11-17: Making Moodle Matter Madly -> Beyond Our "Mermaids" Socratic Seminar -> Re: Beyond Our "Mermaids" Socratic Seminar
by - Monday, 18 October 2010, 08:38 am

While I agree with Jonah and Thalia that we've discovered discrepancies between individuals' definitions of greatness, I think that perhaps (as has been suggested before) our class ought to try and reach some sort of consensus on what greatness is, if only for the sake of discussion. It would be interesting to try and agree on a single definition, seeing as everyone seems to have such different ones. If this seems too difficult, maybe we could try to agree on what the writer of the piece we're discussing means when he uses the words "great" or "greatness" and use that definition for our discussion?

Show parent | Edit | Split | Delete

See this post in context

Joan shared this dilemma and the documentation (the video clip of the Socratic seminar and subsequent Moodle reflections) with a group of colleagues meeting regularly to explore documentation as a tool to support group learning. In talking to her colleagues, Joan came to realize that consensus not only might not be possible, but it also might be less important than she had imagined. What was key was that students engage more deeply with each other's thinking. This meant creating activities that demanded deeper listening.

The Greatness Interviews

From the personal writing students did online at the beginning of the course, Joan already knew whom and what they admired and why. Thalia admired self-sacrifice for the benefit of others and suggested that greatness is the ability to rise above extraordinarily difficult circumstances rather than intellectual or other capabilities. Jonah admired artistic excellence. Joan did not want these perspectives to get lost. Thalia's and Jonah's ideas referenced two kinds of hard work—the work of striving for a better life for loved ones and of sacrificing for one's art.

Joan wanted her students to take more responsibility for understanding one another's perspectives more deeply so she asked them to interview each other about the origins of their ideas about greatness. She then asked them to write up their interviews

in short essays that would be shared with the whole class. Joan asked a colleague to help videotape the interviews. Joan suspected that video would more compellingly communicate the emotional dimension of the students' ideas and that having students watch the video would foster their authentic consideration of one another's ideas.

Based on revisiting their interviews on video and in writing, students generated thirty-three generalizations about greatness that represented some level of agreement (specifically, those statements that were made by at least two students). Ultimately the group reduced the statements to fourteen and plotted their degree of agreement as their **"temperatures"**—the high numbers representing strong agreement (or "hot") and the low numbers representing strong disagreement (or "cold")—on **"greatness fever charts."** Violet insisted that the group create a comment column because **"we might be giving the same rating for different reasons."**

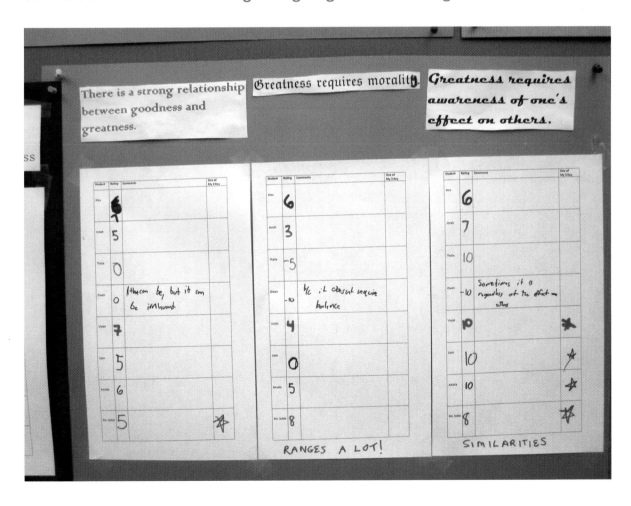

Although students were willing to revisit what they agreed to and why, Joan wondered if they were merely clarifying their thinking or actively questioning it. Two days after the fever chart activity, Joan asked the class if they felt their discussions about greatness were worthwhile. Thalia, who was videotaping that day, was first to name a benefit.

Thalia: *I think it's made us more open-minded but I don't really think it's, like, dug us out of our hole.*

Joan: *What do you think of the relative value of the two things you just mentioned?*

Thalia: *There are more things that we look at now, that we consider, when we talk about greatness . . . we're taking all of those things into consideration.*

Liam: *I've started to see more and more ways to approach this topic. I think it's impossible for us to decide one sole definition of greatness. I just don't think that's ever going to happen.*

Jonah: *Yeah, but I definitely agree that I've opened up my opinions because when we first started talking about greatness . . . I wasn't even thinking about being, like, a moral person and having . . . goodness in your heart. I was just thinking about being great at something—working hard. But now . . .*

Alex: *I was exactly the opposite.*

Joan: *Say more.*

Alex: *I didn't think about being great at something.*

Joan: *So maybe that's the biggest thing we've achieved is this kind of willingness to concede that there are two ways that people look at greatness, and some people look at it both ways, both in terms of character and in terms of [achievement]. We don't agree about the amount that they're related to each other but we do agree that they both exist.*

Despite the students' claims of open-mindedness, Joan again wondered whether they really entertained one another's ideas so she shared excerpts from Thalia's video with her colleagues. The adult group was struck that students seemed to be arguing more for the sake of thinking than winning. Students seemed not only to exhibit tolerance but also to expect murkiness and complexity. Were Joan's colleagues' interpretations right?

Joan shared a fifteen-minute clip from the adults' conversation on the last day of class to solicit students' reactions. This led to the following discussion, which Joan felt reflected new insights about the thinking and learning process and the importance of multiple perspectives for understanding one's own and others' viewpoints.

Liam: *Greatness was a big exploration for us . . . A lot of . . . teachers put a big topic out there, but this was different. You had more strategies, so it felt much more open to me. It wasn't that you were trying to get us to think a certain way or define greatness a certain way; it was more that you . . . wanted us to think about certain things. Ultimately, all of us were allowed to have our own ideas.*

Alex: *In a lot of classes, you have to spend time figuring out what the teacher wants you to think so you can give it back to them . . . so it stops being about your thinking.*

Violet: *What also happens is that teachers want you to come to a common definition or a consensus about something, and since that's what the teacher wants, people's thinking gets lost.*

Owen: *For an AP class, this went so far. This class taught me how to think . . . It was so much more than test prep.*

Liam: *But like someone said on the video, we really did come to care about greatness.*

Owen: *We sort of got invested. The topic got to mean more and more to us. But I was impressed by how far we went beyond greatness. We learned a lot more about the thinking process and about how to learn . . . how you sort of go about thinking about something.*

Joan: *Actually, this is what I hoped would happen for you. I know I kept . . . muddying the waters. But I wanted . . . you to have the kind of clarity that comes from muddied waters kind of calming down and having things settle out of them.*

Thalia: *But even with what you were doing, I felt that I could have my opinion. I had to think about other people's opinions, but I could express my opinions and still keep them . . .*

Alex: *. . . there wasn't something [in particular] that you wanted here. You wanted my thinking . . .*

Joan: *But that's what I had to learn from you guys. I started the term thinking we could come to some consensus about greatness. The real goal was to have everyone really know what they thought, and what everyone else thought, and why—so everyone had to think about everyone else's thinking before being sure about their own. I also started out the year thinking we might not have enough diversity of opinion [in a small class], but I was wrong about that, too. Each of you had lots of facets. I think it was Violet who pointed out that even when we agreed on things, we agreed for very different reasons. So what did that agreement actually mean? So even though we have no consensus, I feel very happy about where we ended up because all of you really understood what each other thought and why.*

Liam: *You have to find a way, Ms. Soble, to make next semester's bigger class have that happen.*

Owen: *Because in this class, we had to know what we were thinking. But in a large class, it gets too easy to be quiet and too easy not to know what you think.*

Joan was pleased with how far they had come as a group. The conversation revealed the role other people's thinking had played in enriching individual thinking. Joan's hope that she could make time in an AP course for developing deep understanding as well as test preparation was realized. However, Owen's last comment tapped into a deep concern. Joan was already worried that students would have fewer opportunities to express their ideas in the larger class the following semester. Owen's comment cautioned that if students had fewer opportunities to express their ideas, they would also have fewer opportunities to develop their ideas. Although Joan knew the experience the next semester was bound to be different—both because the class would be larger and the students would be different—she resolved to continue creating an environment in which students were both enticed and required to develop their thinking in negotiation with others.

Chapter 4

The Amazing Circus Act
Making Visibility Part of the Equation in High School Mathematics

Teacher

Doug McGlathery

Students

Joan Brunetta and Nora Spear

This learning portrait describes how two tenth grade students' efforts to make their learning visible via a public display further their own and others' learning.

It was Nora who asked their teacher, Doug McGlathery, if the girls could work on their project out in the hallway. Nora and her tenth grade partner, Joan, were nearing the end of the "high dive" unit in Doug's interactive mathematics program at Cambridge Rindge and Latin School. The girls arrived at a daunting equation after weeks of hard work investigating and developing understandings about trigonometry, quadratic equations, and components of velocity. The equation corresponds to the question **"At what precise moment would a person, dangling by their ankles from a Ferris wheel, need to be released in order to fall safely into a cart of water traveling on a straight track under the wheel?"** As with previous classes, once students arrived at the correct equation, Doug assigned them the task of writing out the equation on rolled paper as a way to emphasize and celebrate the enormity of this intellectual feat.

As the girls embarked on their task, Nora bemoaned the fact that, as high school students, they never got to work out in the hallway as they had in elementary school. It was a way of working that, for her, seemed not only practical (the final length of the girls' display equation was twenty-five feet long, making it hard to maneuver in the small classroom) but also served an important social-emotional function. In Joan's and Nora's words:

Joan: *In high school, you're usually in an assigned seat and you never get to move around. I don't know if it's just more fun to get to move around or if it helps us in some other ways. We just feel more comfortable.*

Nora: *It's just nice to work in the hallway. If someone walks by, they probably know you and they talk to you and ask you what you're working on. As opposed to high school where, if you're in the hallway, the security guard is like, "Get to class." It's just different. It's nice to feel like that's our space.*

Doug agreed to their request and the girls worked on their project out in the hallway for the next several classes. As Nora predicted, their work captured the attention of friends and other students who passed by. What the girls and Doug did not predict were the additional opportunities for learning that emerged from making the girls' work more visible—through the creation of the display itself and through doing this work publicly.

Showing the Thinking behind the Equation

When Joan and Nora began the work of writing out the equation, a task they initially thought would be purely technical, they began to realize that they had forgotten much of the meaning behind it. They had figured out each of the individual parts along the way but, when it came to putting it all together, they no longer remembered which phrase corresponded to which part of the overall problem. They needed a way to make sense of the smaller equations within the larger equation so they came up with the idea of color-coding them. In Joan's words, **"Math isn't as 'sticky-in-your-heady' as some of the other subjects. When we color-code[d] it, we relearn[ed] it. Having it that way made it easier to see and easier to remember."**

Although the move to color-coding was initially for themselves—helping them to remember what each part of the equation referred to—they quickly realized that this strategy could help others understand it, too. This gave a new impetus to the task at hand. Nora and Joan now wanted to go beyond the initial assignment to create a poster-sized version of the equation that they were making for Doug. They decided to create an exhibit that would remain in the hallway, showing the thinking behind this problem and helping others to understand the equation, too.

Nora: *Each number or symbol in the equation represents something on the Ferris wheel, like the speed or the height or something. Things reappear multiple times, so we made each thing a separate color so that each time it appears we keep it the same color. Then we have the key that says, **"If it's this color, it's the speed."** So you can see how all the parts fit together.*

Because of the equation's length and complexity, the girls didn't have enough different colored markers to distinguish its various components so they came up with additional ways to delineate them through a system of underlining using different patterns. As they worked to break down the equation in this way, they began to understand it in a way they hadn't before.

$$(9w) + (7.85 \sin(9w)) \left(\frac{7.85 \cos(9w) + \sqrt{(7.85 \cos(9w))^2 + 64(57 + 50 \sin(9w))}}{32} \right)$$

Joan: *Having the color-coding helps to see the connections and importance of things. You can see patterns, like what's showing up the most, and the layers of the equation. Like the bars . . . there are smaller bars that represent sections that are being multiplied by another number that's color-coded and then, all together, that makes a larger bar which is something else. It helps you to see, for example, that that last long part is the quadratic formula.*

Nora: *When we made it the first time, we were just kind of breaking it down, step by step to sort of make it manageable. Then we went back to it and we could step back and say, "Okay. Now how does this all fit together and how do the different pieces relate?" We hadn't been able to see it from that point of view before.*

Doug was impressed with the creativity the girls exhibited in their attempt to break down the complexity of the equation into conceptual chunks. In his words, "I found this . . . particularly powerful because it showed that they were doing some high-level abstracting of this expression [which is] one of the biggest ideas, if not the biggest, in mathematics."

"Is Eight Feet of Water Really Deep Enough?"

Once Joan and Nora decided that their equation poster and color-coding scheme would be part of a larger exhibit for other students in the school, they began to create the context necessary to bring others more fully into the problem. First they made a legend to explain their color-coding system. Next they began to write out the problem

Legend

Numbers

■ = Starting X position of cart

■ = Cart's speed (ft/s)

■ = Ferris Wheel's speed (ft/s)

■ = Ferris Wheel's angular speed (degrees/s)

■ = Wheel time (seconds)

■ = 4ac (see quadratic formula)

■ = Distance from center of Ferris wheel to cart

■ = Radius of wheel

■ = 2·a (see quadratic formula)

Underlines

■ = Initial upward velocity of diver (as a function of w)

▨ = Distance from diver to cart after w seconds

▨ = Falling time for diver as a function of w

■ = Total time (wheel time + falling time)

■ = Total distance cart traveled (as a function of w)

▨ = Final X coordinate of cart (as a function of w)

▨ = X position of diver at point of falling (as a function of w)

▨ = Horizontal velocity of dive (as a function of w)

▨ = Divers final X coordinate (as a function of w)

▨ = Horizantal distance traveled by diver during fall (as a function of w)

□ = Time diver should begin fall

the equation was created to solve, along with a panel that included vital information that Doug had provided such as the starting position of the diver, the radius of the wheel (50 feet), the time it takes for the wheel to make a full turn (40 seconds), the speed of the cart (15 feet per second), and the depth of the water in the cart (8 feet).

Friends and other students passing through the part of the hallway where they were working became interested in their project and stopped to watch and ask questions, occasionally even challenging Nora and Joan's responses. Doug videotaped some of these exchanges. A particularly spirited discussion ensued about whether eight feet of water—the depth of the water in the cart specified by the girls in their problem statement—would actually be enough for a person to survive the fall. Because the depth of the water had been "a given"—one of the few parts of the problem that the girls had not had to figure out for themselves—they hadn't given it much thought until that moment.

Their friend's question got them wondering so Joan attempted a reply, **"I think there are ways to slow yourself down in the air and water."** But their friend remained unconvinced and Joan and Nora were left feeling they had more to figure out before they could finalize their display.

Doug suggested that he, Joan, and Nora visit the physics teacher, John Samp, thinking that he might be able to shed light on their question because of his disciplinary knowledge. As it happened, John had a friend who was a former stunt diver and knew a lot about the tricks divers use for falling into shallow pools of water from great heights and the physics behind them. So the girls left armed with new ways to support their argument.

An Eye on the Audience

Throughout the process of creating their display, Joan and Nora were constantly trying to take on the perspective of their audience—high school students not in the interactive mathematics program. Although components such as the color-coding and corresponding legend were intended to help their audience from a conceptual standpoint, Joan and Nora realized that they needed to

THE AMAZING CIRCUS ACT — the Problem Statment

We have all gone on a Ferris wheel, but we haven't been dropped from one! In this circus act a performer is traveling on a huge Ferris wheel while being dangled from their ankles. A cart is traveling on a strait track so it will pass under the wheel. The goal is for the man to be dropped and fall into the water instead of to his death. But at what point is this? Thats exactly what we had to find out! We had to consider speed, distance, gravity, time, and inertia and we ended with one big Equation!

pique their audience's curiosity as well. After all, they had put so much work into their display—they wanted people to actually read it! The ability to take on the perspective of a potential audience is another way that having a partner helps.

Each girl came to the project with unique skills and perspectives. Although Joan had more experience taking advanced mathematics courses than Nora and brought more content knowledge, Nora's self-awareness as a learner enabled her to look at their work from the perspective of someone who might need things explained more clearly.

Joan: *The thing about having stuff in the hallway is that people never really look at stuff in the hallway. I want to think that people will stop and look at [it] but Nora is more realistic about things . . . I think sometimes I [take the] complicated route and Nora is, like,* **"People aren't really going to look at this"** *and suggests ways to make it simpler.*

Nora: *I think I'm just kind of like that. I'm always [saying],* **"No one is going to understand what you're saying . . . We need to make it clearer."**

Their keen attention to communicating clearly led the girls to create a title and problem statement that they hoped would capture their audience's attention. To reflect the drama of the situation, they decided to highlight the idea that mathematical precision can actually become a matter of life and death.

In assessing the girls' work, Doug said, **"I think it reflects an understanding that even when you are restating or reframing a problem, making it . . . engaging is of primary importance, especially when . . . making a first impression."**

The Not So "Final" Display

After Joan and Nora's display had been up for a few days, Neuza Defigueredo, a precalculus teacher whose classroom is around the corner from Doug's, invited Joan and Nora to present to her class. Neuza admired the girls' work in the display and the deep understanding it reflected. She also saw an opportunity to help her own students see the relevance of the math they were learning by having Joan and Nora introduce them to the "real world" example of the Ferris wheel. As Joan said, **"[As an engineer] my dad had to relearn math. He knows all the math, and he was good at it, but he didn't learn why you would ever want to use it. This [approach builds in] situations it can be used in. Not that a Ferris wheel is a very common situation, but you know what it's about, so then you can think about this is like this."**

Joan and Nora were excited and a little nervous about the prospect of teaching another class. Doug gave them time in class to prepare. They developed a plan to bring much of the material they created for their display with them. Doug reflected on some of the intelligent teaching decisions he saw the girls make, **"One of the most clever things they did was to take the diagram they had written dimensions on and cover each piece of information with a sticky note [so the other students would need to do some thinking of their own]. I was very impressed with how engaging they made their presentation,** inviting the other students to participate from the very beginning, unveiling the numbers they had covered up as the need for them was realized."

At the end, Joan and Nora summarized the key understandings that led to solving the unit problem and took the class around the corner to see their big equation in the hall. They used the visual hints of color and underlining of conceptual phrasings to engage the students further, asking them questions they had prepared ahead of time. When they were done, the pre-calculus students applauded. Afterward, Joan commented, **"Once we made the presentation, I felt like we really knew it all the way through."**

Neuza told Doug later that the students liked it so much they asked when they would get to do something like this. Neuza, feeling motivated to identify more opportunities for her students to apply the concepts they were learning, suggested, **"Maybe my class could present to yours next time."**

Chapter 5
Meet the Directors
Kindergartners Study the Boston Marathon

Teachers
Ben Mardell and
Rachel Bragin

Students
Christopher, Rosie,
and Simon

This learning portrait explains how two teachers support a small group of five-year-olds as they plan, prototype, and film a ten-minute video about the Boston Marathon to share with other students, family members, and the larger community.

There were just four school days left until the première of their film, and members of the video planning committee—Simon, Christopher, and Rosie—were hard at work. Along with one of their actors, Alex, they clustered around a video camera, reviewing footage of the scene they had just shot—a reenactment of the arrival of the helicopter that signals to the crowd below the approach of the elite runners in the Boston Marathon.

Christopher, Rosie, and Simon had been preparing for the shoot all morning, planning the scene, recruiting actors, and preparing them for their roles.

In reviewing the footage Rosie noticed that Christopher had zoomed in on just one of the actors and suggested, **"I think we need a little bit more Marcus. And Jason."** Christopher agreed. They shot the scene again and returned inside to plan the wheelchair racers' scene.

Ready, Set, Go!

In spring 2004, the two kindergarten teachers at the Eliot-Pearson Children's School*—Ben Mardell and Rachel Bragin—led eighteen kindergartners in a study of the Boston Marathon. Most of the children in Ben and Rachel's class had never heard of a marathon before. However, Ben had long been fascinated with the race and hoped his enthusiasm for the topic would be contagious.

In the months preceding the marathon, the teachers traveled the racecourse (by car), read about the history of the race, and brainstormed ways to engage the kindergartners in studying the marathon. The teachers introduced the investigation of the marathon three weeks before the day of the race. Activities that emerged from the children's questions and interests included the following:

- Meeting race participants and asking them questions such as, **"Why are you running a marathon?"**
- Transforming the dramatic play area into a gym to train
- Conducting research on the web to learn the names and nationalities of runners
- Running around a football field to get a sense of how long 26.2 miles really is

*The Eliot-Pearson Children's School is a laboratory school at Tufts University in Medford, Massachusetts. The school's five classes serve seventy-eight children, three to eight years old. Families reflect a variety of structures and cultural, ethnic, and linguistic backgrounds. As an inclusion model school, Eliot-Pearson works closely with school districts to serve students with special needs.

On "Marathon Monday," the teachers, most of the children, and their families attended the race together. Children learned the reason for the hovering helicopters, cheered the runners on, observed medical workers caring for a dehydrated runner, followed the progress of the race on the radio, and expressed awe at the vast number of cups left discarded on the street.

The Genesis of the Committee

A week later—their first day back in the classroom after the marathon—the teachers and children looked at photographs and video of the marathon as a way to include those who had not been able to attend and to refresh their memories about the day's events. Afterward, the group brainstormed ways they might share what they had learned about the marathon with the school community. After much discussion, the children decided to make a book, a sculpture, and a video. Rachel and Ben wanted the children to take the lead in communicating what they learned and organized three planning committees to spearhead these efforts. After hearing an explanation of responsibilities, Christopher, Rosie, and Simon volunteered for the video planning committee.

Over the next month the three five-year-old videographers met several times a week during the daily choice time to plan, organize, and shoot the video. To help launch their first session, Ben asked the group to review a list of important aspects of the race generated by the entire class the previous day. The list included: it was a long race, everyone who finished got a medal with a unicorn on it, and the runners threw their cups on the ground. As a committee the children decided which aspects of the marathon should be included in the video.

Creating a Storyboard

The video planning committee's second session began with a review of a short film made by Christopher and three other classmates earlier in the year to illustrate the idea of storyboarding. The earlier movie, inspired by *The Lord of the Rings*, consisted of four clips. Ben pointed out the thumbnail pictures in the video program that represented each part of the movie. He also sketched a picture of each clip to demonstrate how filmmakers create storyboards. Then Ben gave the group a stack of paper on which to draw their scenes and several long strips of blue construction paper on which to lay out their

scenes. Rosie asked, **"What if we don't know what scenes to draw?"** Ben suggested that she think about what would come first in the video and encouraged her to discuss her ideas with Simon and Christopher. Then Ben excused himself, letting the children know he was available if they needed assistance.

After referring to a diagram on the wall of runners stretching, Christopher, Rosie, and Simon each began by drawing runners stretching. Then they took their completed drawings to the long shelf where they had laid out the strips of blue paper. They placed their drawings in sequence on the blue paper, counted the number of scenes left to draw, and returned to the table to discuss what to work on next. Once the topics were chosen, the children worked quietly on their drawings and repeated the process anew.

After drawing runners stretching, Simon drew a dehydrated runner, Rosie added the starting line, and Christopher drew a helicopter. Next, they all drew runners running. Simon then pointed to a photograph of Kathryn Switzer who, in 1967, became the first woman to compete in the Boston Marathon. Drawing Switzer and her running companions presented a challenge for Simon.

"She has a hard number," he said, pointing to the number *nine*. **"I don't know how to make that number. Do you know how?"** he asked Christopher. Christopher nodded and showed Simon the difference between a six and a nine. Once this drawing was placed on the blue paper, Christopher and Simon counted the spaces that remained. Excited by their progress, Christopher called out, **"Six more to go. Let's do it!"** Returning to the table Simon pointed to another photograph on the wall and announced, **"I'm going to make that wheelchair guy!"** Christopher was skeptical. **"Oh man! That's going to be so hard."** Simon remained resolute, **"But I can still do it."** Rosie called out in support, **"Me, too!"** Swayed by their enthusiasm, Christopher declared, **"Try it! Let's go! Let's do it together, okay?!"** Finally only one space on the blue paper remained. **"You're going to finish it, Rosie,"** Christopher exclaimed as Rosie filled the last blank space with her drawing—runners who are happy because they have finished the race. Christopher draped his arm around Simon and the boys counted up their drawings—nineteen in total. The trio called Ben over to show him their work. They had spent over thirty minutes on this project.

Feedback from Friends

A few minutes later, Christopher, Rosie, and Simon were seated in front of their fifteen classmates, explaining their storyboard and soliciting feedback. Amelia suggested they add the water cups on the ground. Simon turned to Rosie and Christopher to find out what they thought of the idea. Gabe suggested that they add 7.2 more scenes so they will have a total of 26.2 (the number of miles in the marathon).

Simon called on Ben.

Ben: I like all the ideas, but I would change the order a bit. What I mean is that you have stretching and then you have a dehydrated runner before the race even starts. I would put the dehydrated runner in the middle of the race.

Evan: Like right here (pointing to the middle of the storyboard)?

Gabe: You mean, in order?

Ben: Yeah.

Simon: But we can do whatever we want because it is our study group.

Ben: Right, but you're trying to make it make sense. That's why you are getting feedback.

Next, Rosie called on Rachel.

Rachel: I have another suggestion. Ben made me think of putting it in order. And I'm trying to remember: when we went to the marathon, which came first, the helicopter or the dehydrated runner?

Simon: Helicopter.

Rachel: So do you want to make it like the real marathon?

Simon: No, first the wheelchairs, then the helicopters, then the runners. The dehydrated runner is in the middle of the race.

At their next work session, the video planning committee used the whole-group feedback to revise the sequence to "make it more like the real marathon" and added a scene about cups on the ground. They also decided that, rather than using actual footage from the marathon, they would ask their classmates to act out scenes for the movie. Using the revised storyboard as a template, Christopher, Rosie, and Simon planned, directed, and shot scenes, such as the one described at the beginning of this learning portrait. The committee laid out a racecourse in the play yard that included a table with water cups, a wagon to transport dehydrated runners to a first aid station, and a finish line. After the committee filmed classmates running the course, the teachers assisted them in editing footage, resulting in a ten-minute video. The movie premiered to a delighted group of family members and classmates.

The Blessings of a Learning Group

Participation in the video planning committee had an impact on not only Christopher, Rosie, and Simon, but also their families. Planning the video led to animated dinner conversations in Rosie's home discussing, for example, how to film the helicopter scene. At Christopher's house the video became a major hit, competing with *Lord of the Rings* for play time. Simon's family continues to attend the marathon, returning to the twenty-mile mark each year. In preparation Simon reads the book he and his classmates wrote to his younger sister, who tells her friends that her brother is a marathon expert.

The impact on the children's parents went well beyond the immediate joy parents feel on seeing their children excited and engaged or their pride on seeing their children's work on display. These parents talk about how the video planning committee influenced how they think about teaching, learning, and children. Rosie's mother, Deb, who teaches four-year-olds at her family child care center, now has higher expectations for her own students. She facilitates long-term projects with the children as "drivers of their learning." Christopher's mother, Jean, feels, "The curriculum will always have a special place in my heart. It was eye opening watching these just-turned five-year-olds talking, negotiating, and thinking things through together. The curriculum pushed them and they met the expectations." Simon's mother, Carmen, refers to the marathon curriculum when giving talks at her church about endurance—not only the endurance of the runners, but also of the kindergartners who, "as individuals and as a group stayed focused on a project that was very big for their age." When she teaches Italian to elementary school children she is most happy when a lesson goes in an unexpected direction because of the learners' interests. Carmen is grateful when her children's teachers take the time to listen to them. She sees being part of a learning group as a blessing.

Chapter 6
Eyes on Engagement
Supporting Student Inquiry in a Fourth Grade Classroom

Teacher
Amanda Van Vleck

Students
Fifth Grade Class
Fourth Grade Class

This learning portrait recounts a teacher's evolving use of documentation to advance her fourth grade students' mathematical, scientific, and collaborative abilities.

According to fourth grade teacher Amanda Van Vleck, **"There is nothing more satisfying than watching a group, large or small, function on its own—solving conflicts, negotiating rules, moving through space, and sharing and revising ideas."** Yet, learning groups need to be nurtured. They require intentionality, practice, the ability to listen and disagree respectfully, and a concern for the learning of others.

Over the seven years that Amanda has taught fourth grade at the Benjamin Banneker Charter Public School,* she has thought deeply about student engagement and how students can take more responsibility for their own and others' learning. She understands that this kind of engagement doesn't just happen; one of the major questions Amanda grapples with is when to step in and when to step out of her students' learning process. For Amanda, consistently providing opportunities for her students to learn in small groups supported by documentation often spawns the kind of student-directed learning she values. The following three vignettes show the evolution of Amanda's efforts to use different forms of documentation to support student inquiry groups.

---

*The Benjamin Banneker Charter Public School is an urban K–6 science and technology school in Cambridge, Massachusetts. Banneker serves more than 350 students, with 92 percent students of color and 82 percent from low-income families.

Spinning Tops

Amanda describes the spinning tops exploration as something that happened **"almost by accident."** The school had implemented a twenty- to twenty-five-minute dismissal period—an open period at the end of the day—that teachers were struggling to use effectively. Always looking for ways to incorporate more student input into the learning, Amanda decided to use this dismissal period as choice time, with a variety of activities for children to choose, including drawing, playing math games, and exploring materials.

One day during choice time, a group of boys began making tops out of the multilink cubes from a collection of materials used to teach math. Sitting at a low table, the boys battled with their tops—spinning them across the table until one top knocked the others off the table. Interest in the boys' idea spread and soon more than half the class was playing with cube tops. The noise—at times approaching pandemonium—was what initially caught Amanda's attention. Although her impulse was to stop the activity, Amanda decided to let the play continue and instead watched, listened, and wrote down what she was observing.

When Amanda looked over her notes, the students' conversations surprised her. Hidden among the crashing, clunking, cheering, and objecting were discoveries, explanations, and provocations for further investigation:

"Mine spins longer than yours."

"Well, yours is lighter than mine. That's why."

"Mine is too tall. It keeps falling over."

"Why don't you take off that cube?"

Amanda was struck by the ways her students were talking about themselves in relation to what they seemed to be learning:

"Look at what I invented!"

"Look at my colors!" (One of the things that most intrigued students was the new colors created by the spinning tops.)

"I started this with Tyshawn and now everyone is doing it."

"Lots of people couldn't spin before. Now they can."

Amanda pondered whether to let her students keep going with their activity and see what happened or to step in and guide them. She decided to intervene in stages and began meeting individually and in small groups with the involved students. Together, they came up with guidelines for the cube tops, including "no battling."

Amanda wondered how she might share some of her observations with her students and how that might influence their learning. It seemed clear that the tops presented fertile opportunities for scientific learning, and the school science expo was fast approaching. Amanda convened a class meeting to discuss possible topics of study. She shared some of the photographs she had taken over the past weeks along with excerpts from conversations she had recorded:

Leon: *Look, Ms. V. Do you see how there's no purple in this? (Leon shows Amanda a top with red and blue and a few other colors.)*

Ms. V.: *Yep. I see.*

Leon: *Watch. (Leon spins the top and a bright purple color appears.) See! Purple!*

Ms. V.: *How is that happening?*

Leon: *(Shrugging his shoulders) I don't know.*

Ms. V.: *Hmm . . . (Amanda waits. Leon doesn't say a word—he just stares at his top.)*

Leon: *I really don't know. (Leon starts to walk away and stops.) Wait! Red and blue make purple! Look at all of the reds and blues! Mr. Kellman (the art teacher) taught me that!*

Ms. V.: *Does that mean you can make other colors, too, using what Mr. Kellman taught you?*

Leon: *Maybe! I'll try . . . Wait. I don't remember anything else he taught me . . .*

Ms. V.: *Hmm . . . maybe someone else does.*

Leon: *Okay! Manuel! Do you remember how to make colors? You know, how Mr. Kellman makes them?*

Amanda then asked her students if they could re-create the story of their top exploration, including what they think they learned and what surprised them. As students gave animated accounts of their discoveries and their puzzles, Amanda introduced new vocabulary to support their learning, such as *diameter* (when students referred to the width of their tops), *axis* (when students referred to **"the part in the middle"**), and *symmetry* (when students described their tops as **"the same on all sides"**).

Later in the meeting, Amanda suggested that the group present their learning from the tops exploration at the science expo, specifying that agreeing would mean the investigation would involve the whole class and it would become a scientific inquiry, including identifying a question and forming and testing a hypothesis. Excited, the students readily agreed.

Once they narrowed down the questions and hypotheses to test, students formed self-selected groups based on the focus of their study. One group decided to continue Leon's exploration of how to create new colors in the spinning tops. Another group decided to explore whether the diameter of the top affects how long it spins. A third group formed to explore the relationship between tops and other things in the world that spin (e.g., merry-go-rounds).

Over the coming weeks, the small groups grappled with their questions, frequently recruiting experts from other teams. For example, the group exploring how diameter affects spinning time developed a hypothesis that someone with more experience can spin a top longer than an inexperienced spinner. They recruited the most and least experienced spinners to collect data.

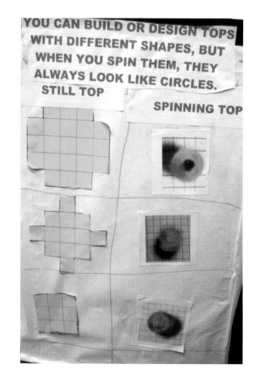

The color group also made discoveries about shape (e.g., no matter the shape when still, a top always appears as a circle when spinning).

They decided to include this finding along with their discoveries about color. The group exploring the relationship between tops and other spinning things concluded that tops and merry-go-rounds must be balanced—the axis must be exactly in the center to spin smoothly, with parts attached tightly so they don't fly off.

When the study concluded, Amanda was left with many questions. How might she facilitate a similar process with her students next year? What materials and routines need to be in place to enable similar kinds of discovery? She ended the year wondering, **"What will be the hook for my kids next year?"** and resolved to remain alert for it.

All Hands In: A Symbol of Teamwork

The following year, Amanda tried videotaping as another way to engage students in learning. Amanda asked her student teacher to videotape a small group during a unit on electricity.

One student, a recently arrived immigrant from Haiti with limited English, appeared especially frustrated, at times walking away from the group when he was being ignored. Another student didn't talk at all; she simply took the materials she needed and worked on her own. A third refused to participate. The student teacher's video revealed one pair of hands in action.

Later that same period, Amanda encouraged the group to try communicating with words rather than just grabbing materials from one another. With Amanda's guidance, the group moved from stalemate to productive engagement. Now four sets of hands were visible.

Two days later, Amanda shared footage from the two stages of the small group's work with the whole class. She asked students to watch the hands at the beginning and end of the clip. Students shared observations such as, **"After Khadija stepped back, Nylea and Faith were all sharing their ideas about what they would do to get the lightbulb to light."** And, **"I noticed that Khadija, Faith, Stephano, and Nylea were all . . . all the hands were moving."** The activity of the hands became a shared symbol of productive teamwork and a successful learning group, and the phrase "all hands in" became shorthand for "good collaboration."

Amanda continued to videotape and share the work of other small groups. By collecting video of a group participating in a literature circle and sharing a three-minute clip with the class without the sound, the students' focus shifted to the behaviors and body positions of students in the group. One student observed that students' eyes and shoulders were turned to the speaker. Another noticed that the students were turning back to the book to reference specific pages and showing each other passages from the text. The class began a routine of reviewing key features of active listening before small-group work.

Amanda also discovered that she could frequently engage students who found small groups challenging by asking them to serve as documenters. Photographing or videotaping active listening and respectful language gave these students a chance to observe what such behaviors look like. The images also served as a guide for their own behavior. At the end of the school year, Amanda posted the class's strategies for group learning in the classroom as a reference for the incoming class. She also shared documentation of students' conversations about working in groups with their fifth grade teachers.

D'Anique's Discovery: Capturing an Aha! Moment in Math

Although videotaping is useful for documenting group learning and prompting detailed reflections from students and adults, it is not feasible to have a video camera running throughout the day. One day, during a math unit on classifying numbers as multiples, factors, even, odd, and prime, Amanda displayed the following riddle on the class's overhead projector and asked students to solve it together as a group:

- I am less than 10.
- I am an odd number.

- I have only 2 factors.
- I am a factor of 14. (Watch out! This is a tricky clue!)

Dionne kicked things off by volunteering to help eliminate numbers on a 0 to 99 chart with a dry-erase marker. As the class neared a solution, D'Anique discovered that the group had overlooked the fact that the number 1 has only one factor. The mistake caught even Amanda by surprise. Only a few students picked up on the significance of D'Anique's discovery.

That night, frustrated that a key learning moment had gone unnoticed, Amanda decided she wanted more students to understand that the number 1 has only one factor. All year, Amanda had struggled with the class plowing ahead in math without thinking critically or monitoring themselves. She wanted students to realize that a lot of thought goes into seemingly simple mathematical tasks and that they are all learners and teachers who can benefit from each other's aha! moments. So Amanda re-created in PowerPoint the comments and questions that led up to D'Anique's insight and presented the slideshow the next day as an "opportunity to travel back in time."

Riddle #3
- I am less than 10.
- I am an odd number.
- I have only 2 factors.

Dionne

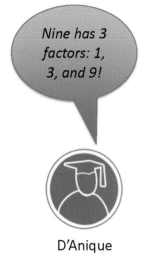

D'Anique

Nine has 3 factors: 1, 3, and 9!

So, which of these DO NOT have 2 factors?

X	1	X	3	X	5	X	7	X	X
X	11	12	13	14	15	16	17	18	19
20	21	22	23	24	25	26	27	28	29
30	31	32	33	34	35	36	37	38	39
40	41	42	43	44	45	46	47	48	49
50	51	52	53	54	55	56	57	58	59
60	61	62	63	64	65	66	67	68	69
70	71	72	73	74	75	76	77	78	79
80	81	82	83	84	85	86	87	88	89
90	91	92	93	94	95	96	97	98	99

Like all teachers, Amanda has always made interpretations. Documentation helped to make those interpretations more robust and often more accurate. It created the visible traces of Amanda's observations and children's learning so they could be revisited. The artifacts of learning generated by Amanda and her students, whether represented by written notes, video clips, or PowerPoint, offered multiple entry points for engaging students in individual and group learning. This type of documentation connects the *what* to the *how* of learning and allows past learning to inform present and future learning. For Amanda, intentional observation was critical:

> *I now see one of my most important teaching roles as that of observer of student-to-student interactions and group play and conversation. I have become a far more intentional observer, looking for patterns of behavior and language use, listening for moments of confusion or sudden clarity, and zooming in on student interactions with each other and their learning. Rather than relying just on curriculum guides or impressions from the day, I base my teaching decisions on the data I collect from careful observation and documentation. I try hard to step back and see where the students lead conversations and learning, and what engages them. This is not to say that I am . . . unaware of my teaching objectives, but the path to reaching those goals is flexible and should respond to the needs and understandings of my students.*

Riddle #3

- I am less than 10.
- I am an odd number.
- I have only 2 factors.
- I am a factor of 14. (Watch out! This is a tricky clue!)

7 is a factor of 14 because 7 x 2 = 14!

Dionne

But wait! One is a factor of 14 too!

D'Anique

Oh! You're right! We need another clue to end up with 7.

Ms. V.

47

PART II: Principles and Practices

In part 2, we describe the underlying principles and practices of making learning visible and situate these ideas in the current context of high-stakes testing and accountability. The chapters are grounded primarily in the learning portraits presented in part 1 as well as the work of other pre-K–12 teachers involved in the Making Learning Visible project. Although the core practices of group learning and documentation are explained in separate chapters, we see these practices as interwoven and mutually supportive.

As you read these chapters, we invite you to consider the following questions:

- What are your core beliefs about learning and how do they shape your teaching practice?
- In what ways do the five principles of learning put forth in chapter 7 connect (or not) to your beliefs?
- How are the five principles manifested in your classroom practices?
- How might you use the practices of group learning and documentation to better support individual and group learning in your classroom?
- How might making learning visible open up new possibilities for meeting standards and addressing accountability in your setting?

Chapter 7
Making Learning and Learners Visible

Think back to a powerful learning moment you experienced when you were a student. Perhaps it was conducting a service learning project or making a compelling argument in a debate or rehearsing for a school play. Maybe it was a chemistry experiment that generated unexpected results or an art exhibition you created with classmates. Almost everyone has such memorable experiences. They stick with us. Now consider: What made this moment so unforgettable? Perhaps it was the knowledge you gained about the subject or something you learned about yourself as a learner. Or maybe it was the kind of relationship you forged with other students or adults or the feelings of joy or surprise that the moment elicited. The power of such moments is that not only do they stay with us as fond memories, but they also shape the way we think of learning and who we are as learners.

The learning portraits in this book offer telling clues about what makes for memorable and profound learning. We argue that during such experiences, who the learners are—individually or collectively—and what they are learning become visible. In "The Yellow Door," kindergartners and their teachers came together to find a creative solution to a classroom conflict that led to a rich, emergent curriculum that included inquiry, data collection, and analysis. "The Vernal Pool" depicted middle-schoolers investigating the hidden aquatic life in a nearby forest and advocating for its protection based on their findings. "Grappling with Greatness" portrayed high school students openly wrestling with their divergent points of view regarding the nature of human greatness. "The Amazing Circus Act" followed two high school students as they explored complex mathematical equations in the hallways of their school. "Meet the Directors" showed a small group of kindergartners creating and producing a short film on a local marathon to be shared with parents and the community. In "Eyes on Engagement," a fourth grade teacher experimented with observing and recording moments of engagement and collaboration to support her students' inquiry. Each of these stories suggests core beliefs about teaching and learning that come into play as students and teachers come to know more about themselves and their subject matter.

The products and processes of the students' and teachers' learning become visible through quotes, drawings, videos, reflections, and photographs. Sharing these artifacts of learning with other students, teachers, and family members often provokes new understandings, curiosity, surprise, and delight. In each learning portrait in part 1, teachers and learners built collective knowledge with their peers and each other. Children and adults actively facilitated and reflected on their own learning as well as the learning of others, becoming resources for peers and colleagues. Each story points to practices that reveal who learners are and what they are coming to know.

This book shares the fruits of more than a decade of work on the Making Learning Visible project carried out by researchers at Project Zero at the Harvard Graduate School of

Education and public school educators and students in Massachusetts and Ohio. We put forth an approach that emphasizes the reflective, social, and artifact-driven qualities of powerful teaching and learning. Such practices are vital for all ages of learners, from early childhood to high school, and for adults as well. At their core, these classrooms make learning and learners visible by drawing on the power of the group and documentation for understanding, deepening, and extending the learning of students and adults.

The Need for Visibility

Although the learning portraits in this book paint a promising picture, much of the learning in today's classrooms remains largely hidden from the view of teachers, students, families, and the wider community. Often, the only representations of learning made public are test scores, grades, and rankings. Such numbers or letters are poor stand-ins for the depth, variety, and complexity of the learning that is—or could be—happening. Too often students and their thinking remain largely invisible. This is unfortunate because classrooms should be places where powerful learning is experienced, demonstrated, and assessed. Yet even when the most dedicated teachers try to create contexts for compelling learning, they confront formidable challenges. Demands to cover content and teach to standardized tests can be overwhelming. Short class meeting times stifle teachers' and students' ability to explore new learning opportunities when they emerge. Even when generative moments that enhance student learning do occur, time is limited for teachers and students to reflect on and make greater sense of that learning. In sum, many classroom practices are simply not aimed at supporting and revealing the depth and complexity of student learning. Like the tip of an iceberg, they provide only glimpses into what lies beneath the surface.

A Brief History

Since 1997, the Making Learning Visible project has investigated the dynamics of individual and group learning and the role of documentation in supporting the development of powerful learning groups in classrooms and schools. From 1997 to 2000, Project Zero researchers collaborated with educators from the Municipal Preschools and Infant-Toddler Centers in Reggio Emilia, Italy. Over the next decade, we worked with teachers and teacher educators in the United States to translate these ideas into US classrooms across schools, subject matter, and age range. The Making Learning Visible seminar was launched in 2003 at Project Zero in Cambridge, Massachusetts. Twenty-one educators representing thirteen public schools and three teacher educators from Wheelock College and Lesley University gathered monthly to make learning visible to each other and in their classrooms. The goal of the seminar was to develop ways to support children's and adults' individual and group learning by collecting and reviewing documentation of how and what children learn. Over time, the group (whom we refer to as Making Learning Visible, or MLV, teachers) grew to include teachers from five of the six learning portraits in this book.

Many of the schools participating in the seminar worked with traditionally underserved populations, and some schools had test scores that were among the lowest in their community. In response to the public outcry from politicians and community members about failing students with the greatest needs, teachers during this time period were under enormous pressure to teach to the state tests. Yet teachers also recognized that relying on traditional forms of teacher-directed instruction was unlikely to solve the problem. In fact, such traditional approaches tended to perpetuate the problem of student disengagement. Forty-five-minute class periods, large class sizes, and teacher-directed instruction were not conducive conditions for creating the types of powerful learning experiences described in part 1.

To fuel their inquiry, the MLV teachers drew inspiration from the pedagogical practices of the Reggio Emilia educators. The Reggio preschools are world-renowned for their extraordinary approach to early childhood education, which has inspired countless public and private schools and centers for young children in the United States and elsewhere. The Reggio approach is based on what educators there call a *pedagogy of listening and relationships*. Reggio educators hold an image of the child as capable and powerful as opposed to unskilled and passive. The Making Learning Visible seminar was grounded in two books: *Making Learning Visible: Children as Individual and Group Learners* (2001), which shared results from the first phase of the Project Zero–Reggio collaboration, and *Making Teaching Visible: Documenting Individual and Group Learning as Professional Development* (2003), which reported on an initial collaboration with eight preschool–middle school teachers in the United States.[1]

For seven years, we, along with other colleagues at Project Zero, facilitated the MLV seminar. Teachers from local pre-K through high schools who were interested in Reggio ideas voluntarily joined the seminar as school teams. These teams supported each other in designing and documenting classroom experiments and providing feedback. Seminar members framed their inquiry around several guiding questions such as, "How do learning groups form, function, and demonstrate understanding?" and "How can documentation extend and make visible individual and group learning?" Through cross-school discussions grounded in artifacts of student learning, teachers developed strategies to make learning and learners visible as a way to shape and deepen subsequent learning. The ultimate goal was to create learner-focused environments that would alter traditional relationships between and among students and teachers.

The learning portraits in this book show students learning to give and receive feedback and pondering concepts such as what constitutes human greatness and mathematical factoring. But they also demonstrate the complex ways in which students individually and collectively develop content knowledge as well as a sense of themselves as learners. Teachers and students come to see themselves and others as competent learners and resources for each other. By the 2010 school year, the MLV seminar had involved more than seventy-five teachers from twenty schools in the Boston area. During this time, we also worked with the Wickliffe Progressive Community School, a public K–5 school of approximately 480 students in Upper Arlington, Ohio. We have worked closely with all of these teachers—and a number of parents—to pilot and document more than thirty innovative teaching strategies that currently serve as the basis for professional development courses and workshops in numerous schools in the Boston and Cambridge school districts. The stories, practices, and tools from this work form the basis of this book.

The Broader Context

Lessons from these schools and similar progressive approaches have produced a variety of ways to make learners' intellectual efforts and evolving identities visible. The MLV perspective shares much in common with the small schools movement, performance-based and portfolio assessments, looking at student work, and problem- and project-based learning. Done well, these and other strategies generate multiple opportunities for teachers to know the learners and for learners to know themselves and each other. However, external forces, such as high-stakes testing, an emphasis on quantitative measurement, and a narrow view of learning can quickly frustrate teachers interested in pursuing such approaches and limit the scope of education to those features of learning that are easily seen.

There are encouraging signs that this is changing. Research and policies on the need to make learners and learning visible are gaining ground. In 2002, the US Department of Education gathered industry leaders, such as Microsoft, Cisco, and Apple, to identify the qualities of schools that will best support the nation's educational needs in the coming decades. Their recommendations culminated in the report, *Learning for the 21st Century*, which highlights the need for classrooms to promote the skills of collaboration, communication, critical thinking, and creativity.[2] They emphasize that learning can no longer be an isolated, individual, teacher-led activity, and instead must move beyond classroom walls to engage families and community members. Teachers and students need learning strategies that provide more nuanced views of the complexity of learning in order to foster such twenty-first-century capacities and skills.

Five Principles of Learning

Every teacher wants students to learn a variety of things in the classroom, from developing number sense in the early years to understanding the nature of "greatness" in a high school literature class. Of course teachers want students to learn facts or equations but rote memorization and recall reflect only one layer of learning. Deeper layers are evidenced by "flexible performance"—students' ability to apply what they know flexibly in novel situations.[3] The stories in this book portray students trying to extend what they know in new and creative ways, guided by teachers who make clear and careful choices about what knowledge and skills are worth learning.

What distinguishes classrooms that make learning and learners visible from other classrooms? Based on close work with teachers, we have identified five core (and often overlapping) principles of learning in such classrooms that suggest powerful learning is purposeful, social, emotional, empowering, and representational. In the following sections, we describe each principle, using illustrations drawn from the learning portraits.

Learning Is Purposeful

As our Project Zero colleague David Perkins notes, an essential feature of powerful learning contexts is that teachers make clear decisions about "what's worth learning."[4] The idea that the learning in classrooms needs to be purposeful might seem obvious. However, in many classrooms, connections from week to week about what is being learned are rarely made, and learners are often unaware of the goals and larger purposes of what they are learning. A number of helpful strategies have been devised to address this situation, such as the Coalition of Essential School's emphasis on "essential questions" to guide the learning experience over longer periods of time[5] and Project Zero's "Teaching for Understanding" framework that stresses the need to create public understanding goals that explicitly focus and connect learning for students and teachers on a daily basis.[6] MLV classrooms share this commitment.

Classrooms that make learning visible, similar to many other effective classrooms, are organized around understanding, knowledge, and skills that are purposeful—relevant to the learner, the teacher, the discipline, and often the larger community. The learning portraits show learning that is shaped by student interest, from curiosity about the shapes and sizes of school doors in "The Yellow Door," to the choice to shoot a movie in "Meet the Directors," to the spinning tops science project in "Eyes on Engagement." In "The Vernal Pool" project, the teachers suggested that students try to get the vernal pool certified in part because they sensed a lack of emotional connection to creating a nature guide the previous year.

Purposeful learning is also shaped by the passions and interests of teachers. The Boston Marathon project was sparked by Ben Mardell's passion for the race, just as Joan Soble's overarching understanding goal stemmed from her desire to explore issues of human greatness. Even though most of Doug McGlathery's (the teacher in "The Amazing Circus Act") colleagues preferred to teach the more traditional mathematics curriculum, Doug continued to teach the interactive mathematics program because of his deep belief in the value of learning math in problem-based situations that resemble the inquiry methods used by professional mathematicians. The disciplines are also a key consideration in teachers' choices of curriculum; teachers often focus on concepts, processes, and skill sets that are central to a discipline. Doug considers the high-level abstracting engaged in by Joan and Nora to be one of the biggest ideas in all of mathematics. In "The Yellow Door," Nicole Chasse asked for input from a math specialist to sharpen students' data collection skills.

Finally, purposeful learning also entails making learning relevant to the world beyond the classroom when possible. Thus, in "The Amazing Circus Act," Nora and Joan worked on complex mathematical equations applicable to a real-world problem, the seventh-graders in "The Vernal Pool" created a guidebook for the broader public, and the top spinners shared their findings at the school's annual science expo.

Learning Is Social

Learning is more than the passive transmission of knowledge from teachers to students. The landmark research and writing of psychologists Lev Vygotsky[7] and Albert Bandura[8] show that the creation of knowledge is not just an individual activity; it also develops in social exchanges with others. In "Grappling with Greatness," high school students shared their divergent perspectives on the nature of greatness in pairs and in large-group conversations. Learning in this classroom went beyond coming to know the ideas that the teacher had in mind or that were reflected in the curriculum guides. Rather, learning involved wrestling with multiple points of view and interpretations, and led to more complex thinking about the material. Meaning emerged from the acts of sharing, reflecting, and revising one's knowledge over time.

These processes involve not only the students and their teachers but also students from other classes, other teachers, and sometimes families and members of the wider community. In "The Vernal Pool," students learned about the various types of aquatic life through close observation and data collection in a nearby forest. They helped one another interpret their field notes and observations to identify patterns and raise questions. Students worked within and across larger groups to build, share, and test their theories. Their teachers also learned together by comparing observations of students' learning in order to design the next steps of the project. To extend the social aspect, the completed guidebook was publicly shared in a local library for other students to use as a resource, and the students' findings were given to local policy makers.

The social principle of learning suggests that assessments about who learners are and what they are learning are not fixed and static statements rendered by an isolated authority figure at the end of a unit. Rather, teachers and students regularly see glimpses of themselves as learners along the way. In "Eyes on Engagement," Amanda Van Vleck shared a variety of photographs, video clips, conversation excerpts, and images with her students so they could observe, interpret, and discuss the challenges of individual and group learning in their class. The students came to see each other as experiencing doubt, surprise, flashes of insight, and perseverance. The students and teacher developed their knowledge of these challenges in public—in the presence of others. The skills and behaviors they identified to better support learning were for everyone to use throughout the year.

Learning Is Emotional

Classrooms that make learning and learners visible develop more than intellectual knowledge and skills; they also develop an emotional aspect of learning. Such classrooms spark emotional connections to content through thoughtfully selected materials, questions, and phenomena. Emotions, when not attended to, can inhibit learning and collaboration. "The Yellow Door" began with the students' and the teacher's frustration about the children's inability to share the wooden door. One could easily imagine how this emotion might lead to further conflict and mistrust, and understand if the teacher simply took control and unilaterally solved the problem. Instead, the frustration was channeled, giving way to elation and pride when the children solved the problem by designing their own, new doors for themselves and future students to use. Their learning process was marked by experiences of joy and wonder as they visited unfamiliar places in the school to find more doors. Similarly, the fourth-graders in "Eyes on Engagement" experienced surprise and delight as they played with spinning tops, frustration during group work, and enchantment when a classmate's aha! moment was re-created. The high school students in "Grappling with Greatness" also reflected on their feelings of confusion and dissonance as they learned to listen more deeply to their contrasting views of "greatness." In each story the teachers, too, experienced surprise and wonder as they paid closer attention to the learners and their learning. Making the emotional component of learning visible played a core role in motivating learning in these classrooms, for students and teachers alike.

Providing or creating high-quality and appealing materials also heightens the emotional principle. The *Life in a Vernal Pool* guidebook pairs stunning illustrations of aquatic life with compelling text designed to spark the interest of the reader. In "The Yellow Door," the wooden doors as well as the process of exploring unknown areas of their school captivated the kindergartners. The choice of medium for sharing documentation can also trigger emotions that motivate learning. Watching videotaped interviews of their classmates speaking openly about their beliefs about greatness fascinated Joan Soble's students and fostered feelings of empathy and closeness.

Teachers who uphold the emotional principle of learning make the familiar unfamiliar and turn the ordinary into the extraordinary. Such classrooms provide opportunities for students to reveal and reflect on feelings of wonder, surprise, and pleasure. These and other emotions have been shown to have a positive impact on factors that support children's and adults' learning, such as motivation,[9] engagement,[10] and memory.[11]

Learning Is Empowering

Teachers who make learning visible encourage students to become more self-directed—taking charge of their own learning and committed to sharing their learning with others. For example, in "The Yellow Door," Nicole Chasse sought children's input to resolve a classroom problem. The idea of designing and building new doors came from the children, who then asked Nicole's co-teacher John, an expert in woodworking, to help them. Teachers like Nicole and John create multiple opportunities for learners to direct their own learning. Over time, students become skilled at setting goals, developing strategies, overcoming obstacles, and assessing their own progress. The importance of cultivating skills for self-guided learning, first identified by the psychologist Malcolm Knowles in the 1970s,[12] has been resurrected recently in such contemporary frameworks as the Partnership for 21st Century Skills.[13]

Teachers who strive to make learning and learners visible watch for opportunities for students to lead their own learning. In "Eyes on Engagement," Amanda carefully observed and chose learning moments that she shared back with students in order to put them in charge of their own learning. These "teachable moments" are re-created in order to support students teaching students. In "Grappling with Greatness," Joan actively pursued students taking responsibility for their own learning, with Joan in the role of guide and facilitator. Many students noted that Joan's approach led them to become more critical thinkers who were able to sit with the complexity of an issue such as "greatness." As one student later commented, "So many connections and realizations can be made through conversations about literature . . . I could have had this realization earlier, but I think something can really be said about coming to this conclusion in a small group of fellow students, with no teacher to guide the conversation."

Teachers become empowered as well. Rather than follow scripted forms of teaching, they decide what is worth learning and how to go about it based on what they come to know about their students. In each of the learning portraits, teachers sifted through their own interpretations of student learning, tested ideas with colleagues, and reshaped strategies for the classroom. The teachers crafted their own questions and goals for their students, along with practices that encouraged and celebrated adults and students as teachers and learners all.

Learning Is Representational

In "The Yellow Door" kindergartners drew designs for their doors, recorded data they collected of the characteristics of doors in their school building, created graphs to represent their ideas, and eventually built and painted colorful wooden doors. The students' learning was enhanced by translating their knowledge into a variety of representations that demonstrated and deepened what they were coming to know about doors. Throughout the process, the teachers collected and reflected on these representations in order to gauge progress and consider next steps.

Learners express and represent their learning in multiple ways. As Howard Gardner suggests in his theory of multiple intelligences,[14] evidence of learning can be demonstrated in a variety of symbol systems beyond the traditional school focus on words and numbers. Reggio educators similarly emphasize the "hundred languages of children" through which children can develop and express their thinking. Pictures, quotes, student work, video, audio recordings, and the like offer glimpses into the complexity of learning and learners. When these representations of learning are shared publicly, they can contribute to building collective knowledge and provide a memory for the group. Teacher Amanda Van Vleck selected photos and videotape to share with her students, which led to episodes and stories that students could recall quickly. With the group of top spinners, Amanda shared her notes of conversations and photographs as a way to engage students in creating a narrative of their learning, reinforcing key concepts and vocabulary in the process. Students can also participate in the process of sharing their learning with others, such as when kindergartners in "Meet the Directors" were invited to choose the format for sharing their learning.

Creating and sharing multiple representations of learning at multiple points in the process allow students to demonstrate and deepen their learning simultaneously. Students' representations of their learning can be shared while work is in progress in order to get feedback that they can use to reshape or rethink that work. Such representations can also be shared on completion of a particular task or project, providing an opportunity for more summative assessment.

Core Practices of Making Learning and Learners Visible

The beliefs that learning is purposeful, social, emotional, empowering, and representational provide a pedagogical basis for making learning and learners visible. In the coming chapters we detail two practices—learning in groups and documentation—that build on these five principles.

Learning in Groups

The idea that group learning is a critical classroom practice has been around a long time. Research in the latter half of the twentieth century established cooperative and collaborative learning practices in classrooms as effective ways to develop skills and knowledge in a variety of age levels and disciplines. Group learning plays a central role in making learning and learners visible by providing the social context in which emotional and intellectual knowledge and skills can be developed. In classrooms that make learning visible, teachers promote learning groups through five interconnected strategies:

- Nurturing students' capacities to learn together. In "Eyes on Engagement," Amanda Van Vleck found multiple ways to help her students collaborate more effectively.
- Designing engaging tasks that benefit from a group perspective. When Nicole Chasse's kindergartners struggled to share the yellow door in the block area, Nicole turned the problem into curriculum that engaged children in problem solving and collecting and analyzing data.
- Facilitating conversations that deepen learning. In "The Vernal Pool," Mandy Locke and Matt Leaf used the group to address misconceptions and for students to give each other feedback and reflect on their work.
- Forming groups intentionally. In "Meet the Directors," Ben Mardell and Rachel Bragin considered the complementary qualities and skills of individual children in order to form hypotheses about the composition of small groups.
- Choreographing individual, small-group, and whole-class learning. In "Grappling with Greatness," Joan Soble's high school students sometimes worked individually and sometimes in small or whole-class groups. The movement between these contexts provided opportunities for learning and reflection.

Chapter 8 will describe these strategies in greater detail.

Documentation

The practice of documentation involves teachers and learners observing, recording, interpreting, and sharing via a variety of media the processes and products of learning in order to deepen and extend learning. Documentation has strong roots in the pedagogical strategies growing out of the Reggio Emilia schools and the assessment strategies of "process portfolios" developed at Project Zero.[15] More than a technical strategy for gathering images or student work, documentation creates new relationships between teachers and learners in the teaching and learning process. Although documentation is most connected to the representational principle of learning, it also connects to the other principles outlined previously in this chapter. Sharing concrete documentation with students and teachers anchors the social process of learning and invites multiple perspectives, interpretation, and theory building. The selection of what to share often entails emotional considerations; for example, whether one wants viewers to experience wonder, surprise, or other feelings. Finally, the act of collecting documentation can heighten teachers' and students' sense of directing their own learning. In classrooms that make learning visible, the practice of documentation has several distinctive features:

- Documentation is often guided by a specific question about the learning process, such as, How do students experience a culture of inclusiveness in my classroom? How do students think about greatness?
- Documentation engages teachers and students in collectively analyzing, interpreting, and evaluating individual and group learning. It requires and is strengthened by multiple perspectives.
- Documentation involves using multiple languages—that is, learners have many ways of representing and expressing their thinking that can be captured in various media and symbol systems, not just speech.
- Documentation is not kept private; it becomes public when shared with other audiences, whether other students, teachers, family members, or the wider community.
- Documentation is not only retrospective; it is also prospective. It shapes the design of future contexts for learning.

Chapter 9 will examine this practice in greater detail and provide specific strategies for understanding learners and learning more deeply.

Often in classrooms, group learning and documentation are decoupled and thought of in isolation from one another. A teacher might focus on structuring a well-designed cooperative learning activity one week. Later, she may consider how pieces of student work from the activity could be collected and shared back with the learners or other teaching colleagues. However, we encourage educators to keep a watchful eye on the features that unite these practices. In combination, the two practices form a powerful and integrated approach to making learning and learners visible.

The five core principles of learning act as threads that will be woven through the chapters to come. The next chapters describe how the two practices of learning in groups and documentation together support making learning and learners visible.

Chapter 8
Unpacking the Practice of Group Learning

Learners are in groups all the time while they are in school but not all these groups are learning groups. In learning groups, members are engaged in solving problems, creating products, and making meaning; students and adults learn from one another by encountering new perspectives, strategies, and ways of thinking. Members of learning groups also learn with one another by modifying, extending, clarifying, and enriching their own ideas and the ideas of others.[1] In such groups, learning is purposeful, social, emotional, empowering, and representational.

As chapter 7 suggests, the promotion of learning in groups has a long history and well-developed theoretical underpinnings. In Vygotsky's sociocultural perspective, learning is inherently social; the internalization of interactions transforms ways of thinking.[2] From birth, learners are guided into ways of thinking, feeling, and behaving by family, peers, teachers, and others. Based in part on these ideas, many elementary classrooms incorporate the practices of cooperative learning. Learners are placed in small groups, assigned specific roles and tasks, and taught important teamwork skills.[3] The goal is to leverage the social dimension of learning to help individuals master well-defined content and skills.

The learning portraits expand on this view of learning groups. Working together is a central part of "The Vernal Pool" project. These seventh-graders collectively figured out how to collect and display data and create the *Life in a Vernal Pool* guidebook. The descriptions, folktales, and watercolor paintings in the book benefitted from peer feedback. Learners referenced work from previous classes to get ideas for their writing and artwork. As the students explained, their work involved "bouncing ideas off friends," "friendly debates," and "lots of revisions." Making the book was an enormous task and emotions helped carry teachers and learners forward. As English teacher Matt Leaf recalled, "It stopped feeling like work. The students' excitement and their gains in writing, self-confidence, and getting along sustained me." The Four Rivers students recalled the excitement and pride in seeing their names in the newspaper after their vernal pool was certified and protected from development.

Solving "The Amazing Circus Act" problem and displaying it in an engaging format is something high schoolers Nora and Joan could not have done alone. Joan contributed her advanced math skills and Nora contributed her capacity to frame problems in ways that were compelling to others. Their work was also supported by people outside the group: a friend's question about the depth of the cart of water led to new investigations. Nora and Joan's desire to connect with others brought their work out into the hall where such interactions could take place. It also resulted in the request to present their work to another class, helping them gain confidence in their abilities to think and act like mathematicians. Nora and Joan's poster not only helped others understand the work but the very act of creating the poster and the use of color-coding to explain the parts of the formula also advanced their own mathematical thinking.

Learning in groups always entails individual learning as well as the learning of the group. Our Project Zero colleague, Steve Seidel, argues the following:

> It is possible to see the group as holding the individual in its arms with care, respect and love. . . . The group that embraces the contributions of each member, however diverse or contradictory, may well provide exactly the right context for the emergence of strong individual identities. Through the debate, experimentation and negotiation that characterize the work of these learning groups, each member comes to see, and in time to value, the particular, even idiosyncratic, qualities of the others. The valuing of each member's contribution means that each person not only develops respect for the others, but also has the experience of being valued for what he or she brings to the problem at hand.[4]

A common reaction to the products and processes of learning in Reggio Emilia and to the learning portraits featured in this book is "Our kids can't do that." Teachers of younger and older students report that groups in their classrooms experience far more disruptive conflict and off-task behavior; students participate much less productively in collaborations and collective meaning-making. Some educators suggest that, because of family structure, socioeconomic status, and cultural background, the children in their classrooms are not capable of such collaboration. And although group work can be rewarding and empowering, the inherent tensions of working in groups make success far from guaranteed. So on one level, teachers who suspect that their students "can't do that" are correct; often, their students cannot collaborate to such a degree . . . yet!

In this chapter, we offer specific, interconnected strategies to promote learning groups. Through analyzing the approaches taken by the teachers in the learning portraits and the methods of other teachers with whom we have worked, we have distilled five general strategies:

- Nurturing children's capacities to learn together
- Designing engaging tasks that benefit from a group perspective
- Facilitating conversations that deepen learning
- Forming groups intentionally
- Choreographing individual, small-group, and whole-class learning

Nurturing Children's Capacities to Learn Together

At the start of our research in US schools, we visited a preschool classroom and shared the visual essay "The City of Reggio Emilia."[5] In the essay three children spend an hour drawing a breathtakingly detailed map of a city. After hearing the story, many children wanted to draw maps of their own. Willingly, we provided paper and pencils. Three boys came together and began drawing on a large piece of paper. They drew quietly and in separate corners, as if there were three separate pieces of paper. Suddenly one of the boys drew large circles that covered his classmates' efforts. Frustrated, the two left the activity. Map-making was over. A few weeks later we visited a sixth grade classroom, again sharing the visual essay. These twelve-year-olds were impressed by the work and collaboration of children half their age. Yet when asked how they felt about working in groups, they were unenthusiastic. As one student remarked, "I do all the work, and they get the good grades."

It is not enough simply to tell a group of learners to work together. Learners must have an interest in understanding other minds and the skills to collaborate.[6] In addition, many students do not perceive themselves as actually *learning* in groups; rather, they think learning takes place when the teacher gives you the answer. Supporting children's reflections on their learning processes is key to nurturing their capacities to learn together. Making the learning processes of groups visible enhances children's metacognitive awareness of how to learn from and with one another. Children learn collaborative skills (e.g., asking for help, providing meaningful assistance) and develop the disposition to work in groups in part by seeing how the ideas and perspectives of others can enrich their own learning. Documenting and sharing learning is particularly useful in creating a classroom culture that supports learning from and with others.

We identify at least three key components of nurturing children's capacities to learn from and with each other: creating awareness of factors in successful group work, grounding conversations about group learning in documentation, and providing adult models.

Creating Awareness of Factors in Successful Group Work

Amanda Van Vleck's ("Eyes on Engagement") proactive efforts to nurture her fourth-graders' capacities to learn together begin at the start of the school year. Amanda engages her new students in conversations about the factors necessary for successful group work, sharing ideas generated by previous classes to jumpstart their thinking. Students discuss effective ways to ask for and give help, the importance of body language in inviting collaboration, and strategies for helping everyone feel included in group work. Amanda keeps a written list of her students' reflections that the learners can reference. Before small-group activities, the list is often reviewed. The class also debriefs after small-group experiences, adding other lessons to the list. Amanda is also alert to finding symbols that capture the spirit of learning from and with others. In "Eyes on Engagement," Amanda used the photograph of the hands of members of a small group working together on a science project as an icon for collaboration. These efforts continue until the end of the school year when students reflect on what they have learned about working in groups in order to provide advice to the rising fourth-graders in September.

Raising students' awareness about the factors that contribute to successful group learning aligns with the empowering principle of learning by giving students the means to take charge of their own learning. Making children's learning visible is also useful when a learning group is not functioning well. Ninth grade English teacher Lindy Johnson found that students in one of her three classes in an urban Massachusetts public school discounted the value of peer feedback, paying little attention to comments classmates made about each other's work. In response, she asked all of her class sections (one hundred students total) to discuss in small groups and then write responses to three questions:

- What did you learn from the teacher today?
- What did you learn from another person's comments today?
- What did you learn from another person's writing today?[7]

As Lindy suspected, two classes generated many ideas about how they learned from others, but the third class's written responses included "I learned nothing from the teacher today," "I didn't learn anything from my peers," "I learned nothing from other people's help," and "[I learned] that they have no life."

Lindy decided to share the responses of the two other classes with this group. As she read,

> [the students] were completely riveted, and this was a class that was never riveted. They were really engaged, I mean, you could hear a pin drop. They were really into this. After I had read both sets of responses, I asked, "Why do you think there is such a difference between your responses and period 6's responses?" Diamond said, "Period 6 paid more attention than Period 3 did. They had a lot more to say, and they weren't so lazy." Jasmine said, "Period 3 said they didn't learn anything because maybe they just already knew some of the things, or maybe they just didn't feel like writing. They just wanted to be lazy." And Kevin said, "Because you do not like this class."

Lindy then asked them why they thought she wanted them to hear other students' writing and if they thought they could learn as a group. To this latter question Paul responded, "I think we can if we really try." Building on Paul's comment, Lindy asked, "A lot of you said we were really lazy in here. Do you want to change that?" The students said they did, leading to a shift in classroom dynamics.

Grounding Conversations about Group Learning in Documentation

Amanda and Lindy used documentation to ground their conversations with students about the value of group work. When the committee planning a book about the Boston Marathon encountered problems, their teachers showed the whole class a five-minute clip of the "Meet the Directors" storyboard session as an example of a successful group. After viewing the video, children reflected on what helped this group learn together. Children noticed Simon asking for help, Christopher offering assistance, and Rosie encouraging Simon in his efforts to draw the wheelchair racer. Inspired by their classmates, and with concrete moves in mind, the book committee's next meeting went more smoothly.

Although asking students to reflect on their own group behavior is valuable, starting the process with personal examples can be risky, especially if trust and respect are concerns. Presenting an example from another setting, like the learning portraits in this book, can be an effective way to nurture students' capacities to learn together. (See tool 2 in chapter 11 for a protocol on how to facilitate such conversations.) Seeing young children work together can be particularly effective. High schoolers encountering such learning groups conclude, "If little kids can do this, so can we."

Providing Adult Models

The adults in a school act as models for learning from and with others and provide a vocabulary for group learning. Throughout the year leading up to the Boston Marathon study, kindergarten teachers Rachel Bragin and Ben Mardell discussed problems and ideas in front of their students (e.g., "Do you think it is raining too hard to go outside?"; "Should we see if the comedy study group wants to get feedback on their work at sharing meeting?"; "I don't think they should present today because Micah isn't here and he knows the most about the play."). Such modeling demonstrates the social principle of learning. During "Grappling with Greatness," Joan Soble showed her students excerpts from the videotape of her colleagues discussing aspects of the curriculum as an example of adults learning from each other's perspectives. Even without videotape or with only one adult in the room, teachers can make their learning from others visible (e.g., "I got this idea from Ms. Merrill."; "Reading Janet's essay really changed my mind.").

Designing Engaging Tasks That Benefit from a Group Perspective

The tasks described in the learning portraits engender a high level of commitment on the part of learners and teachers. Students give up recess and stay after school to work on these projects. Also, because of the tasks' scope and complexity, rarely can one person accomplish them alone.

The learning portraits are grounded in what teacher educator Rachel Lotan at Stanford University calls "group-worthy tasks."[8] Such tasks are open-ended, have multiple entry points, and benefit from different perspectives to reach solutions. They foster a sense of purpose in the group. Learning extends well beyond the individual mastery of skills to individuals becoming part of something bigger than themselves and contributing to their communities. Group-worthy tasks address meaningful topics for children and adults and have the potential to engage all learners.

Meaningful Topics for Students and Teachers

Meaningful topics can arise from individual or community conflicts, student questions that connect to important learning goals, or compelling student or teacher interests. "The Yellow Door" project was the result of an ongoing conflict in the kindergarten block area. Rather than solve the problem by getting rid of the offending prop, Nicole Chasse took advantage of the opportunity to develop curriculum through which children learned to solve a community problem along with building math skills. Questions are another source of meaningful topics. When her seventh grade students wondered why the vernal pool did not fill up with leaves, science teacher Mandy Locke saw an entry point into the idea of food webs. Knowing the key concepts and standards they want students to encounter, teachers can be alert to questions, misconceptions, and interests that foster this learning.

Student or teacher interests and passions are also a rich source of topics. Teachers who are passionate about a topic convey an excitement for inquiry that can be contagious. In "Meet the Directors," Ben Mardell chose the Boston Marathon because of his own passion for the race, whereas the specific areas of study were chosen because of students' interests—for example, focus on medical care for runners grew out of several children's interest in becoming doctors.

Finding a group-worthy task can be challenging. Mandy Locke and her colleague Matt Leaf spent a great deal of time reflecting on past projects in developing the vernal pool curriculum. In previous years, they had used curriculum that addressed state standards such as studying endangered species around the world or the animals of the Connecticut River Valley (where the school is located) but always felt something was missing. After much discussion, they realized that focusing on one location, advocating for its protection from development, and creating a guidebook was exactly the right scale for seventh grade students.

The philosopher David Hawkins cautions teachers facilitating group inquiry to ensure that all learners are engaged.[9] Hawkins argues from a moral perspective that teachers need to reach all students but pragmatic considerations are also germane because disengaged students can distract the group from the task at hand. An entry-point chart is a useful tool here. Teachers (ideally with colleagues) create a simple grid with the class list. They then go through the list, considering questions such as "What is this student's interest in the topic?" and "What strengths would this student bring to this small group?" Students can also participate in this process, providing their own answers to these questions. (See tool 4 in chapter 11 for a more complete description of entry-point charts.)

Topics for Adult Inquiry Groups

Identifying meaningful tasks is just as important for adult learners engaged in inquiry. As part of a year-long MLV course at the Baldwin Early Learning Center, a pre-K through first grade Boston public school, we asked teachers to select the parts of their practice they most wanted to explore. Based on this input, we formed small inquiry groups (e.g., children's storytelling, promoting health and wellness, etc.). At the end of the year, participants rated these groups as one of the most meaningful parts of the course. The next year, the teachers lobbied for study groups. Now facilitated by the teachers themselves, study groups have become a central part of professional development at the school. (See tool 12 in chapter 13 for a protocol for identifying a question to focus adult inquiry.)

Facilitating Conversations That Deepen Learning

Engaging tasks generate different kinds of conversation among students, whether planning conversations, conversations to generate or puzzle through ideas together, or conversations in which students give each other feedback. The idea to create a video about the Boston Marathon emerged from a whole-class discussion about how the kindergartners could share their learning with the community. Later, feedback from the whole group helped the small group to modify the sequence of scenes in the video. Peer feedback was also central in creating the vernal pool guidebook. Such conversations enable learners to hear multiple perspectives and enhance the planning, meaning-making, and revision process.

Yet good conversations are not automatic. As Joan Soble realized, even for her high-achieving AP English students, close and careful listening was difficult. One British study found that the primary forms of talk in elementary schools around the world are rote, recitation, instruction, and exposition.[10] Academically productive talk (or *accountable talk*—a term first coined by cognitive scientist Lauren Resnick) is more likely to be grounded in discussion and dialogue rather than instructional or expository talk.[11] Resnick argues that accountable talk supports student learning across economic, social, and linguistic backgrounds. Developing a vocabulary of collaboration; using tools such as protocols, thinking routines, rubrics, and norms; and focusing on building collective as well as individual knowledge are all ways to foster such learning conversations.

Developing a Vocabulary of Collaboration

Teachers can introduce relevant vocabulary to support students' collaborative conversations early on. MLV teacher Melissa Tonachel helps her kindergarten and first grade students by introducing key words and phrases such as *inspire* and *How did you . . . ?* As her students build in the block area, paint, and write, Melissa is alert to similarities in their approach. When she notices children learning from and with another, she comments, "It looks like you are being inspired by each other. Are you talking with each other about what you are doing?" Melissa structures whole- and small-group conversations so children can talk about their own and classmates' work. She begins by asking questions such as "Where did that idea come from?" "How did you learn to do that?" and "Is there something in someone else's drawing that you wish you had included in your own?" Melissa helps the class talk about their own and other children's work by introducing phrases such as "I was inspired by . . . ," "I notice . . . ," "Another way you could do it is . . . ," "I wonder . . . ," "Maybe . . . ," "How did you . . . ," and "What if . . ."

Protocols, Thinking Routines, Rubrics, and Norms

Protocols, thinking routines, rubrics, and norms are effective ways to support a variety of conversations. Protocols provide a predictable and safe context to open up work and ideas to inquiry.[12] (See tools 8 through 10 in chapter 12 for documentation discussion protocols for adults.) Thinking routines are short, easy-to-use strategies designed to become part of classroom life and deepen thinking.[13] (See tool 5 in chapter 11 for two frequently used thinking routines—see-think-wonder and the ladder of feedback.) Instead of judging work ("I like it"; "It's good"), children are engaged in observing, describing, thinking, and wondering. Rubrics are explicit, agreed-on dimensions to assess learning that can promote productive conversation and guide critique. Rubrics make learning expectations clear by identifying criteria for what counts in a piece of work and gradations of quality for the criteria; they blur the line separating instruction and assessment.[14] Finally, norms support productive conversations by creating explicit expectations for discourse. Useful norms vary by setting. In some contexts, "It is OK to disagree" signals to learners that offering different perspectives promotes learning. In others, "Monitor your airtime" alerts learners to leave room for all voices.

Giving and receiving feedback can be a particularly sensitive conversational form. Learners need ample opportunities to practice giving and getting feedback, and teachers need to trust that learners can offer useful comments. Successful feedback requires receptivity on the part of those being critiqued and skill on the part of those providing critique. Norms can lower the perceived stakes in providing feedback. The norm "You don't have to follow the advice" can increase learners' receptivity to critique. Acknowledging that not all comments need to be accepted or acted on allows those providing the critique to take risks. Educator Ron Berger suggests three rules for effective feedback: "Be kind. Be specific. Be helpful."[15] Other useful feedback practices include beginning with a quiet time for noticing and thinking; asking—and sometimes preparing—the artist or author to speak first and then remain silent until the end of the discussion; asking a friend to stand with the presenter; and making the benefits of feedback visible to learners.

Building Collective Knowledge

Many cooperative learning and other group learning techniques are still seen as teaching strategies to raise individual achievement. However, the focus of learning in learning groups can extend beyond the learning of individuals to create a collective body of knowledge. Building collective understanding entails putting individual ideas into circulation for discussion, comparison, elaboration, and possible modification by the group. Sharing and advancing the knowledge of the group reflects the "purposeful" principle of learning more directly than the more typical school experience of carrying out a series of discrete activities and tasks. The teachers and students in the learning portraits were engaged in creating products (a video, a book, a set of doors, an equation) that had a life beyond individual students and often the classroom itself.

Structuring opportunities for collective input and output can also be useful for adult learners. At the Lee Academy Pilot School in Boston, we facilitated ten meetings over the course of the school year among preschool and kindergarten teachers. Each meeting featured teachers bringing documentation from their classrooms to get advice from their colleagues on supporting children's narrative development. To provide continuity across the meetings and capture the teachers' emerging understandings, we created a document that collected the insights and promising practices of the group. Over time, teachers added to and modified the ideas in the document. It became a reference for teachers—especially the next year when conversations about narratives were no longer fresh in their memories.[16] (See tool 7 in chapter 12 for facilitation guidelines for adult study groups.)

Forming Groups Intentionally

Although small groups are a particularly useful context for sharing ideas and making collective meaning, they constitute a tiny proportion of most classroom instructional time. One study of the experiences of more than one thousand US first, third, and fifth grade students found that approximately 90 percent of their classroom time was spent in either whole-group activities or independent seatwork.[17] Small groups can bring together learners with shared interests, facilitate listening, and encourage the sharing of multiple perspectives. In "The Yellow Door," Betel's aha! moment about graphs occurred because of the in-depth dialogue she was able to have with Ava—a dialogue that would be unlikely to take place in a whole-group setting.

It can be difficult for teachers to give up direct supervision of student learning. Teachers sometimes worry that the ideas developed in small groups may be wrong, that conversations will go off topic, or that learners won't be able to work through moments of confusion and discord. In classrooms where groups are not running smoothly, teachers often cut back on small groups, leading to a downward cycle. Without an opportunity to work in small groups, learners cannot improve their skills or form the relationships needed for groups to work well, hence, the importance of forming groups intentionally.

The members of a group are instrumental to determining its success, so putting thought into how small groups are formed is likely to be time well-spent. Each member's level of engagement, ability, and desire to work with peers, as well as the interaction between capabilities and the demands of the task, influence the productivity of the group. Although there is no simple recipe for forming groups, group learning expert Elizabeth Cohen notes that research provides some guidance. For example, mechanically grouping by demographics (e.g., if a third of the class is Asian American including one Asian American in every group of three) can be problematic because it risks activating stereotypes and status issues that might get in the way of learning.[18] Heterogeneous groups are particularly helpful for those with lower academic skills and generally do not hold back individuals with advanced skills. In addition, they can foster children's metacognition and ability to understand other minds. However, heterogeneous groups can face resistance from more skilled students or their parents, who worry their children will be "held back" by working with less skilled and seemingly less motivated peers. Our argument is not that there is never occasion for skill-based groups. Yet careful consideration of the factors mentioned in this chapter such as the nature of the task, the choreography of individual and group learning, and intentional formation of the group can increase the likelihood of success of heterogeneous groups. At a time when skill-based segregation occurs as early as kindergarten,[19] we think a greater balance between homogenous and heterogeneous grouping is called for.

Reggio educators have identified several factors to consider when forming groups, including familiarity and friendship (trust being an essential ingredient in collaboration), balancing competencies and skills, and children's interest in the task.[20] Size of the group also matters—as group size expands, the opportunity for individual children to share ideas decreases. The Reggio educators find single-gender and mixed-gender groups operate differently, though the relationship between gender and groupings changes as learners enter adolescence. (See tool 3 in chapter 11 for further considerations in forming small groups.) Here we highlight two key strategies for forming successful small groups: careful evaluation of learners' needs, strengths, and interests, and incorporating learners' input.

Groups Based on Teacher Assessment of Learners' Needs, Strengths, and Interests

Although many of the principles of learning come into play when considering the needs, strengths, and interests of learners, the purposeful and emotional are perhaps the most notable. Shared interest or passion is a critical component of successful small groups. But the relative weight of different factors depends in large part on the purpose and nature of the task. In "Meet the Directors," Christopher, Rosie, and Simon worked long hours planning the marathon video. The trio's willingness to forego the dramatic play and blocks areas was, in part, a result of the intentional formation of the group. Their teachers noted that although the children were not close friends, they knew each other and got on well. Simon was outgoing and brought a contagious enthusiasm to projects he was involved in. Rosie was skilled at helping groups reach consensus, and Christopher had previous experience making videos. They seemed like a good mix, a hypothesis quickly confirmed.

At the Antilles School in St. Thomas, toward the end of a two-month study of the coral reefs surrounding the island, kindergarten teacher Thames Shaw decided to form small groups of students to share what they had learned over the course of their study. Thames's goal was to create groups in which each child could flourish. She had observed that five of her students were intrigued by making small things; they liked to write tiny letters and draw tiny pictures. Thames challenged these five children to create something that would convey the beauty of the coral reefs and why they should be protected. The quintet worked happily and diligently on a small-scale sculpture about the reefs and the creatures that live around them. Thames created a second small group by placing a boy she wanted to help feel more confident with three children she knew would encourage him to share his ideas and expertise. Together, the group made a sign with instructions about caring for the reefs. In a third group, Thames brought together three girls whose literacy skills were just emerging and a boy with solid literacy skills who often acted as a cheerleader for his peers, encouraging and celebrating their efforts. Thames hoped that he would help the girls to practice and consolidate their skills. Thames asked the group to make a list of all the creatures they knew lived on the reefs. At the boy's suggestion, one of the girls used a hundreds chart to assist her in writing the numbers to keep track of their growing list. The group's biodiversity list eventually reached thirty-five as they sounded out *sand dollars, crab, starfish, and squid.*

Incorporating Learner Input

A key factor in the success of the video-planning committee was that Christopher, Rosie, and Simon all volunteered for the job. At the start of a new science unit on horseshoe crabs, Amanda Van Vleck ("Eyes on Engagement") decided to enlist her fourth grade students in the process of making small groups. To launch the conversation, she showed the class video footage of a small group from a previous unit to reflect on what learning in groups looks and feels like. Amanda then asked her students how they would want to form groups for the unit. Opinions were mixed: the majority of students wanted to choose their own groups, some wanted the groups randomly formed, and a few wanted Amanda to decide. In the course of the conversation, it became evident that the children who wanted random or teacher-chosen groups were worried that they would be rejected or picked last if children chose the groups. Amanda challenged the children to think about how to take care of all their classmates and, after a half-hour long conversation, they opted to create the groups themselves with a commitment to include everyone. To accomplish this, they requested the option of forming groups with three or five members (not just four), so they could easily include an extra student or split into two smaller groups. In contrast to the previous week's teacher-assigned small groups in the science lab (which Amanda described as "largely unproductive and disruptive"), the student-formed groups were more focused and collaborative.

Over time, children come to understand that selections should be based on good working relationships, not simply friendship. Reflecting back on "The Yellow Door" project, Ava explained, "Sometimes it is hard to work with a person . . . because everything turns out her way or I do all the work in most of the things. But I think Betel is a good partner for me because she did some of the work and I did some of the work, and she didn't take over and I didn't take over."

Choreographing Individual, Small-Group, and Whole-Class Learning

Different contexts support different kinds of learning. Time on one's own enables learners to practice skills, clarify thoughts, and reflect. Whole-class conversations can foster a whole-group identity; generate a wide range of perspectives on a topic; supply energy, purpose, and feedback to individual and small-group projects; and are necessary when the entire class needs to be involved in a decision. As discussed previously, because of their size, small groups are particularly valuable in supporting listening and meaning-making conversations.

Intentionally choreographing the movement among these contexts is central to supporting individual and group learning. Giving children and adults individual thinking time before they participate in small-group or whole-class brainstorms often leads to more productive conversations.[21] During whole-group discussions teachers can ask learners to turn and talk to a classmate. Whole-class meetings provide important opportunities for individuals and small groups to share their emerging ideas, receive feedback and new points of view, and contribute to building collective knowledge. When students work independently (e.g., on individual drawings or writing assignments), teachers can ask them to pause, circulate around the room looking at classmates' work, and then return to their own work with the possibility of including ideas gleaned from their observations. If small groups become deadlocked, soliciting input from other small groups or the whole class can be more effective than teacher input. Deliberate planning, thoughtful use of technology, and extending teaching and learning beyond classroom walls all enhance the choreography of student learning.

Deliberate Planning

The teachers in the learning portraits artfully plan and choreograph the movement among learning contexts based on the needs of the learners and demands of the project. Matt Leaf began the process of his seventh-graders writing species descriptions for "The Vernal Pool" book with whole-group conversations about good writing. From these conversations, Matt and the students created a rubric that individual students used to guide their work. The rubric provided a basis for small-group feedback sessions that enriched the descriptions.

To help her high school students grapple with the concept of greatness, Joan Soble invited them to work in small groups to interview each other about the origins of their ideas on the subject. Students then wrote individual essays about greatness. Later, Joan used these essays, along with the videotape of the interviews, to launch a whole-group conversation about different views of greatness.

In "Meet the Directors," the teachers frequently gave the students opportunities to think independently and then bring their ideas together (e.g., drawing scenes and then placing them on the storyboard). Christopher, Rosie, and Simon also shared their ideas with the whole class to receive feedback, influencing decisions about how to organize the video. Although the committee generally worked without strife, choosing a name for the video was an exception. Input during a whole-class meeting helped the group break its impasse.

Technological Support

Technology also supports the choreography of learning contexts. Web-based videoconferencing and other communication tools allow individual and groups of students with shared interests to come together from different classrooms, schools, and geographic locations. Such access opens up new avenues for supporting and sharing learning within and across groups. Social media tools that facilitate group conversation, such as Twitter, also allow for greater interaction between and among students and teachers. These tools provide a forum for students and teachers to make and record comments, pose and answer questions, identify connections, and clarify misconceptions. Doug McGlathery, the instructor in "The Amazing Circus Act," uses the online course management system Moodle in a statistics course for eleventh- and twelfth-graders. Doug often asks students to continue classroom conversations using a feature of Moodle called "Q & A." The move from individual thinking to group conversation is built into the program; students must post a comment before they can see and respond to classmates' comments. Doug's students say the tool supports and expands their in-class learning. One student explained, "Having some time to go back and think about it again does change your perception . . . In class, if someone is arguing with you it's more heated. Then you can go home and form your thoughts, maybe form them in a better way and be more convincing, or you'll discover new things about it."

Beyond Classroom Walls

Choreography of individual, small-group, and whole-class learning can also extend beyond classroom walls to parents, administrators, teachers and learners from other classrooms, and community members. These groups can provide information, offer new perspectives on a topic, and serve as friendly audiences for ongoing and completed work. In "Grappling with Greatness," Joan Soble reviewed some of her students' work with colleagues. She then shared her colleagues' impressions with her students using videotape. In "The Yellow Door," Nicole Chasse brought her students to look at graphs outside the fourth grade classroom to inspire ideas about how to organize data. The work of the children in "Meet the Directors" was motivated by the desire to share with their families what they and their classmates had learned about the Boston Marathon. Families can also be brought in at the beginning of a unit (sharing resources and aspirations for their children's learning) or during a project (providing feedback and expertise). (See tools 17 through 21 in chapter 14 for different ways to involve families in supporting student learning.)

Participation in learning groups creates lasting memories about curriculum for young people. Now in second grade, Ava describes "The Yellow Door" project as "very special because that was a once-in-a lifetime chance and no other kindergarten class got to do that." Mandy and Matt's former seventh grade students, now juniors in high school, are surprised by how much they remember about the vernal pool project, recalling with pride how they protected an important natural resource for their community. And Nora and Joan rank their work on "The Amazing Circus Act" problem as one of their most meaningful high school experiences.

Chapter 9
Unpacking the Practice of Documentation

Documentation is not a new concept. Many educators familiar with the term often associate it with data collected for assessment and reporting purposes. Documentation is also used across other disciplines and has business and technical applications as well. Much of what is considered documentation purports to be objective. We define documentation as the practice of observing, recording, interpreting, and sharing through a variety of media the processes and products of learning in order to deepen and extend learning. One similarity between this and more traditional definitions is the belief that collecting and examining tangible artifacts from an experience is a valuable form of research and communication. These physical traces allow others to revisit, interpret, reinterpret, and even re-create an experience. A fundamental difference is that we see documentation as serving not only historical, referential purposes, but also shaping experiences to come.

Our definition of documentation contains more verbs than nouns; this is intentional. We put less emphasis on the stuff collected—the observational notes, photographs, video, or student work—than on the activities of documentation. Although what and how one documents is key, even more critical is understanding that documentation is not an end in itself. In order for documentation to be useful, teachers and learners must actually do something with it. Teachers use documentation practices to deepen learning—their own, their students', their colleagues', parents', and even the larger public's.

Documentation: Not Just a Beautiful End Product

Teachers who initially encounter practices of documentation tend to get stuck on the idea that documentation means taking a lot of pictures or making beautiful panels. Why? Perhaps the magnificent visual essays and panels created by Reggio educators have become a model for what documentation should look like. These powerful visual essays can be overwhelming in their richness and sophistication, not to mention the time required to create them. But they do not represent the full range of what documentation can be. Much of this documentation has been developed to shape educational practice and public perception of children, teaching, and school on a larger scale; it provides only glimpses into how documentation is used to guide teachers' decisions and to shape and deepen learners' understanding.

Yet focusing on documentation's rawer forms—the photographs, recordings, notes, student work, and the like—can also lead to confusion unless teachers are collecting these materials for a purpose. Those who are new to documentation often approach it from a more traditional view—as simply "recording what we did." Documentation is not just retrospective but also prospective. It doesn't just show others what happened but is, first and foremost, for the benefit of the learners as they move forward.[1] Without an understanding of how documentation can serve learners and shape learning while it is underway, teachers are often at a loss about how to get started. They typically struggle with questions about when and what to document and what to do with the documentation once they have it. The answer to all of these questions is this: it depends.

When Is Documentation?

One reason these questions are difficult to answer is that documentation has the potential to serve many purposes and audiences over the course of a learning experience. Focusing on the purposes for documenting helps teachers decide what kinds of documentation to collect and how to shape it for a variety of audiences. (See the tools in chapter 13 for further guidelines on collecting and sharing documentation.)

Many teachers find it helpful to organize visually the when and for whom of documentation. Figure 2 presents a matrix of the contexts in which documentation can be used to make learning visible in order to deepen and extend it. The four quadrants highlight the different purposes documentation can serve for different audiences at various stages of the learning process. These purposes do not fall neatly into one quadrant, hence, the dotted lines between quadrants. For example, the same documentation used to support learners' reflections during a study (top-left quadrant) could later appear on a bulletin board, sharing their learning with others (bottom-right quadrant). Documentation is largely about building connections—temporal, relational, and conceptual—and communication. When documentation serves these purposes, it blurs the lines between who is inside or outside the learning group and when learning experiences begin and end.

For this graphic to be fully useful, we need to define what constitutes "inside" and "outside" the learning group and "during" and "after" the learning experience. Members of a learning

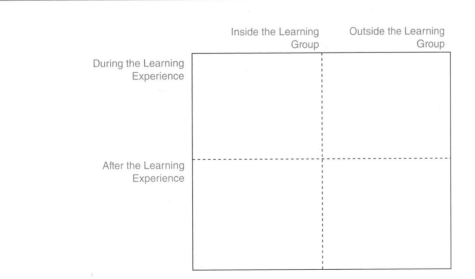

Figure 2. Documentation in Four Contexts

group will differ depending on the situation. Generally speaking, "inside the learning group" includes those most actively engaged in the learning at hand and "outside the learning group" is virtually anyone else.

Similarly, whether documentation falls in the during or after context can shift depending on how teachers define the learning experience. Learning can take place in a single activity, a week-long unit, a two-month project, or a semester-long class. Whatever the duration, learning activities are often intended to culminate in something—understanding a new concept, acquiring a new skill, or creating a product that reflects learning. Everything that leads up to that something falls into the during realm. Not all documentation will run the gamut of all four quadrants, nor does it need to in order to support learning.

To illustrate these contexts, let's revisit "The Amazing Circus Act":

- Inside the learning group included Joan, Nora, and their teacher, Doug. When documenting, the teacher or adult becomes a learner as well.
- Outside the learning group included the other students in the school, the physics teacher, the precalculus teacher and her students, as well as everyone who encountered the final documentation of Joan, Nora, and Doug's work. This last group included Doug's teaching colleagues and others who attended a year-end exhibition in which an exhibit based on this project appeared, teachers at MLV workshops where Project Zero researchers have shared this work, and the readers of this book.
- During the learning experience included all of the ways that Joan and Nora's work was made visible while they were working on it that fed back into the learning process—the display they created in the hallway and the videotaped conversations Joan and Nora had with their classmates that led to new questions to explore.
- After the learning experience included all of the instances of sharing the documentation after Joan and Nora's project was completed—their final display in the hallway; Joan and Nora's presentation to the precalculus class; the exhibit Joan, Nora, and Doug created for their school's annual exhibition of student and teacher learning; and the learning portrait in this book.

Some teachers wonder whether there should be a before column for revisiting documentation prior to beginning a new activity, study, or academic year, such as the planning discussions of the teachers in "Meet the Directors." However, because that documentation came from a previous learning experience, it is included in the after quadrant, which can also be considered before the next time.

Four Key Practices of Documentation

The definition of documentation at the beginning of this chapter and the learning portraits in this book suggest four core practices that teachers, students, and others can engage in across contexts to support and communicate learning. In this section, we explore each of these practices more closely, identifying several strategies within each and the learning purposes they serve.

Observing: The Very Heart of Documentation

In every classroom there are an inordinate number of things to which teachers must pay attention—the content and pacing of group activities, whether students seem to understand the subject matter, which students are engaged and which are not, and on and on. It is no wonder that, even with all the details and activities teachers manage to track from moment to moment and day to day, there is much that they miss. Understandably, teachers often act on their best guess of what is going on.

Stepping Back and Observing with a Sense of Curiosity

In classrooms that make learning and learners visible, teachers try to slow this fast-moving river of information by stepping back and observing with a sense of curiosity. Teachers often consider the first moment they are able to step back and just watch as their first breakthrough in practicing documentation. Joan, the teacher in "Grappling with Greatness," noted, "It's a big move in teacher development when teachers begin to pay more attention to their students than to themselves." Indeed, colleagues in Reggio Emilia often speak of documentation as "a mental attitude" as well as the act and artifacts of documenting.

In "Eyes on Engagement," Amanda identified her first aha! moment while observing a small group playing with tops they had constructed during choice time. What first captured Amanda's attention was the unusually high volume in the room and the students who were running from group to group, apparently off task. Her initial instinct was to tell the students to settle down and get back to work. Instead, Amanda tuned in to some of the small groups' conversations. What she heard pleased her immensely. One group was enthusiastically calling out the colors they saw as they spun their tops—colors that were different from the tops at rest. One boy left his group to compare notes with another about how the size of the top seemed to affect spinning time. The students were so excited about their discoveries that Amanda decided to support further experimentation.

When, instead of providing answers and directives, teachers take a step back and observe, they begin to ask themselves questions such as "What is going on here? What feels surprising about this moment? What does this tell me about what my students know and care about?" The first step to developing curiosity and letting questions become guides is to remain open to the unexpected and to question one's assumptions. Becoming more conscious about noticing the unanticipated moments in the classroom can provide insights into the identities of students as individuals and as a group, the nature of the learning that is unfolding, and promising new directions for teaching.

An effective strategy for beginning a practice of documentation is noticing moments when things are going unexpectedly poorly or well and observing closely what is happening. (See tools 12 and 13 in chapter 13.) The emotions in the classroom—joy, excitement, confusion, and even conflict—are important indicators of the quality of the learning experience. Tuning into them can challenge teachers' assumptions about the nature of the learning and learners in the classroom. When teachers stop and notice which students are involved, what they are saying or doing, and what they seem to be thinking or feeling (as well as their own thoughts and feelings), they sharpen their ability to recognize and respond to the conditions in their classroom and the roles students play in more informed—even novel—ways.

Keeping open to the moment is challenging but crucial. Stanford researcher Pam Grossman notes that the ability to challenge predefined conceptions of their students is a marker of teacher growth and a key behavior in effective professional learning communities.[2] Harvard psychologist Ellen Langer's research suggests that this ability to be flexible in one's mental models is the cornerstone of mindful practice.[3] Stepping back and just watching also shifts teachers toward other observational foci and more focused inquiry.

Focusing Attention through Intentional Inquiry Although the willingness to be surprised and remain open to the unexpected is vital, engaging in intentional and purposeful observation is also important. Observations (and the collection of documentation, which is discussed in the next section) can be guided by specific questions that inform decisions about when and where to look and at whom. Teachers who make learning and learners visible formulate questions about learning to hone their knowledge about the processes of learning and effective teaching. Intentional inquiry often begins with questions that connect to the five principles of learning, such as "What sorts of learning will be most purposeful for me and my students? In what ways are the social aspects of learning contributing to, or perhaps inhibiting, students' learning? How are students emotionally experiencing the content and the processes of learning? What happens to student learning when students are asked to communicate their learning to others (representational)? How can teachers help students become more self-directed in their learning (empowering)?"

In "Meet the Directors," Ben and Rachel decided to let the children take more ownership of the learning process after observing a small group's ability to solve problems without adult intervention. One focus of their inquiry was the type of structures that enable children to work in self-directed groups, such as the storyboard. This experiment then became the focus of the next observation (documented via videotape), allowing Ben and Rachel to enter a cycle of inquiry and continuously hone the supports they provide.

Identifying a hypothesis as well as questions helps advance teachers' thinking and structure observations. In "Grappling with Greatness," Joan began with the hypothesis that her students might be confusing tolerance of different opinions with authentic contemplation of different points of view. This led Joan to question how to deepen her students' engagement with each other's notions about human greatness—a skill valued not only by Joan but also articulated in the state core standards.[4] Although her focus remained steadfast, Joan developed new, yet related, questions, such as "How can I ensure that all students' voices are heard? How important is it that we reach consensus? And, how rigorously are students listening to each other?"

In each example the teachers' questions guide how, what, and when to document in order to support student learning. Formulating a question helps focus and limit data collection and sharpens the analysis. Although observing with an open mind and intentional inquiry may seem like odd bedfellows, together they form complementary entry points to deepening one's understanding of teaching and learning through documentation.

Recording: Capturing the Processes and Products of Learning

The strategies teachers use to capture the processes and products of learning are an important component of documentation. What teachers record from their observations serves as the foundation for the other practices of documentation—interpretation and sharing—and is key to further exploration and knowledge building. Documentation "objectifies" the intangible manifestations of thinking and understanding. Although the word *objectify* often has negative connotations, we use the term to describe the practice of turning something abstract into something concrete. Robert Kegan, a psychologist and professor at the Harvard Graduate School of Education, suggests that the ability to know something relies on shifting that "something" from "subject" (something looked through, like a lens or filter) to "object" (something one is able to look at).[5] In the shift to object, the knowledge becomes something that can be thought about and acted on. When knowledge is no longer such a part of us that we remain unaware of it, we gain the ability to affect it in some way. By creating tangible artifacts, documentation provides new vantage points on learning, often bringing the social and emotional principles of learning to the fore and allowing learners to build connections over time.

Collecting Tangible Artifacts Creating tangible traces of an experience allows teachers and learners to see what was previously experienced from another perspective—outside of oneself and the immediate experience. Without documentation, teachers and learners default to memories of what they think they experienced. But relying on memory poses clear limitations—one can only remember and attend to so much after the fact. Inherently, much is missed. And what we do recall is easily reorganized to fit with previously held theories and assumptions.

Documentation helps develop the subject-object awareness Kegan speaks of and engages learners in developing metacognitive skills. In "Eyes on Engagement," the group-work video was shared with learners, enabling them to view themselves and their interactions from an outside perspective and reflect on what was going on in those moments. By revisiting a moment of struggle—particularly one with which other students could identify—students were able to take a step back to consider things such as the difficulty of the task and the effectiveness of their behaviors and strategies for that situation. These perceptible traces and the conversations around them help learners better understand their actions and how they might continue or modify them in the future.

Tangible artifacts serve a similar function for teachers. Teachers are often surprised by what they see themselves doing or saying—things they were unaware of in the moment. Amanda and several of her colleagues developed a practice of looking at documentation together. Getting an outside view of themselves by watching videotape was enlightening. One teacher, Suzannah, was struck by how much she heard herself talking during activities she had intended to be student-directed. She created a plan to work on talking less. Another colleague, Rachelle, noticed that a student whom she regularly considered "off topic" was consistently responding to questions she had posed earlier. She realized that some students needed more time than she had provided to respond to her questions.

Collecting documentation in different media allows for multiple kinds of listening, eliciting different recollections, insights, and feelings about an experience. (See tools 14 and 15 in chapter 13 for further guidelines.) Different media also tap into the different ways people learn and help level the playing field for a diverse group of learners. Within and across the learning portraits in this book, teachers and students collected a wide range of media that supported and revealed learning in different ways. In "The Yellow Door," photographs enabled the children to remember and share with the larger group the doors they found on their door hunts. The children's drawings and graphs gave their teachers a window into their abilities to represent what they saw and organize information. Videotape of students' interactions, such as Ava and Betel's process of creating their graph, revealed not only the nature of their understanding but also the social and emotional aspects of their learning, such as the joy of both girls when Betel arrived at a new understanding.

Images, voices, sounds, and other perceptible traces from an experience can evoke emotions as well as intellectual thought. By tapping into the emotional aspect of students' learning, the teachers in the learning portraits adjusted the content and process of learning for their students. The video Amanda collected in her classroom allowed students to recall the frustration they felt regarding the difficulty of the task and lack of cooperation and motivated them to think about ways to collaborate more effectively in the future. Joan used the power of students' voices in representing their thinking and feelings on video to encourage deeper connection among her students.

Images can be particularly useful in supporting communication among young children. Betsy Damian, a kindergarten teacher at the Tobin School in Cambridge, Massachusetts, was intrigued one day when she observed all of the children in her class spontaneously, and without a word, begin a group project during recess. The children began forming snowballs and placing one next to another along the big cement wall that surrounded their playground until they had lined the entire wall. Her curiosity piqued, Betsy took photographs that she shared with children the next day, and asked them to explain. The children explained, "We were lining up snow." "Lining up" was a concept with which children were becoming familiar. They were told to line up for lunch, recess, and before going home on the bus. The children's recess activity was a way for them to exert their own power over this process. Betsy was particularly struck by how the photographs engaged all of the children in the discussion, which had never happened before in this group of predominantly English language learners with little shared language. Betsy gained insight into the children's thinking and how visual documentation could support verbal language development. Betsy made a small book out of the images and put it in the classroom library. Children took the book out frequently, using it to recount their story to each other. (See figure 3.)

Figure 3. Lining Up Snow Photo Book

Documentation supports the social principle of learning by communicating the importance of the experiences captured, the knowledge gained, and those who participated. Analog and digital photo albums, home videos, and social media platforms all reinforce our sense of connection to various communities. Documentation serves a similar function in the classroom, helping students and teachers connect to each other as learners and human beings.

Serving as "Memory of the Group" Tiziana Filippini, a senior pedagogista for the Reggio preschools, refers to documentation as "the memory of the group." Few travelers would consider taking a trip to a new place or attending a significant event without a camera. This is because later the photographs help them remember the experience, often evoking aspects that the photographs did not capture. Perhaps because school is part of teachers' and students' everyday lives, the same impulse to preserve experiences is not typically present. Yet, when teachers focus on capturing the critical, and all too ephemeral, processes of learning, they and their students can serve as memory keepers for the group, making it possible to revisit, celebrate, and include others in these experiences later.

Gathering or creating artifacts that remind children of their earlier experiences can deepen learning, particularly for young children. Capturing and revisiting moments from key learning experiences provide continuity and help learners maintain the interest and momentum that deeper explorations require. "Meet the Directors" resided within a larger study of the Boston Marathon that began months before Simon, Christopher, and Rosie's video project. Teachers Ben and Rachel documented throughout the study to help children remember and build on earlier experiences and sustain their interest in the topic over time. Ben helped the planning committee of directors get started on their project by sharing the list of key aspects of the race generated by the whole class at the end of the project's first phase. The documentation reminded the group of things to include in their film and their purpose—to share what they learned.

Documentation is a bit like a time machine, giving teachers the chance to go back to experiences and, in a sense, do them over. Reviewing documentation reminded Ben and Rachel of questions children raised during the conversation when they first proposed the study. The children had been puzzled about how far 26.2 miles was and speculated about whether kindergartners could run that far and whether they would end up in China if they did. The teachers recognized the missed learning opportunities in the children's questions and hypotheses and decided to go back to explore the concept of distance. Ben and Rachel played the video of the conversation for the children before suggesting they go outside to try running 26.2 miles to experience for themselves what that feels like. Most children collapsed on the ground after running two laps around a large field. When their teachers told them they would need to run one hundred laps if they were running a marathon, the children's incredulity revealed their deeper sense of a marathoner's challenge. Revisiting documentation lends relevance to what comes next and, when what comes next emerges directly from learners' own questions and ideas, learners see they are contributing to the direction of their learning.

Documentation supports inclusiveness and participation by filling in gaps for learners who miss central components of a project. In the Boston Marathon study, several children were unable to attend the marathon itself. Because the event represented the culmination of months of study, Ben and his colleagues were careful to document aspects of the event that the class had deemed important. When the children returned to school, video clips and a slideshow from Marathon Monday were played in the classroom. Children who attended the marathon referred to the video as they recounted the experience for friends who had missed it. In "The Yellow Door," not all of the children were involved in every component of the project. To keep the class informed and to keep open the option of taking part in later activities, Nicole made it a regular part of morning meeting for children to share work from the previous day. In "Eyes on Engagement," Amanda's initial idea to document D'Anique's aha! moment stemmed from knowing many students had missed it and wanting them to benefit from D'Anique's insight.

Students develop greater awareness about the value of remembering pivotal experiences when teachers make recording them part of the classroom culture. Involving students in the documentation process enables students to identify moments they want to remember and seek ways to accomplish this. Teachers invite students to be alert to important discoveries or insights to capture and, when appropriate, provide students with the resources to document for themselves. In "The Yellow Door," the children decided what they wanted to remember about the doors they found and invented ways to record the information—through drawing, writing, or asking Nicole or John to take photographs. Involving students extends what teachers can do. In "Grappling with Greatness," it was primarily Joan's students who videotaped group conversations.

The first two practices of documentation—observing and recording—provide the stuff that we call documentation. But for documentation to deepen and extend learning, teachers need to do something with the documentation they collect. The next two sections describe the practices of interpreting and sharing documentation to support learning.

Interpreting: Supporting Reflection That Informs Instruction

The practices of observing and recording conversations and activities in the classroom allow teachers to understand their students and what they know in new ways but they need to make meaning of what they and others see in the artifacts they collect. Interpreting documentation is essential to the practice of documentation and what distinguishes it from display. Reggio scholars George Forman and Brenda Fyfe point out that displays become documentation when teachers assume a research stance and collect documentation that invites inquiry about children's thinking and predictions about effective teaching.[6] As we shall see in the last section of this chapter, when teachers include their analysis and interpretation of the learning represented in the documentation, documentation moves from informing to educating.

Unfortunately, interpretation is a practice that often gets overlooked. Although there are a number of reasons for this, we highlight two here. First, interpreting data in this way involves a paradigm shift for many teachers. Increasingly, the formal assessments adopted by schools ask teachers to record observations devoid of personal judgment. There are times when attempts at objectivity are important. However, when the purpose is to uncover assumptions, know learners better, and examine teaching practices, teachers need to articulate their own thinking and compare their interpretations with those of others (including students). Interpretation reflects the empowering and social principles of learning by honoring teachers' and students' voices and teachers' knowledge about students. The second reason the practice of interpretation is rare is the perennial challenge of time. Here are three specific strategies that help teachers interpret documentation and use the insights they gain to support their own and their students' learning:

- Grounding individual reflection and interpretation in documentation
- Interpreting documentation with colleagues
- Interpreting documentation with learners

Grounding Individual Reflection and Interpretation in Documentation

Interpreting documentation helps teachers develop the observational skills described earlier in this chapter—looking through the dual lenses of open-minded curiosity and focused inquiry. Many teachers use documentation to extend what they are able to see and hear in the classroom by placing audio or video recorders in places where they can't be physically present. They often express surprise and even delight when they revisit the documentation and see that learners are able to stay on task, help each other, and direct their own and others' learning without a teacher present. This knowledge influences the decisions and moves teachers make in the future.

In "Meet the Directors," Ben was surprised on viewing a videotape of a student group creating medals for the marathon runners earlier in their study. When differences of opinion arose and threatened to derail the group's work, Ben noticed that the children were able to resolve the conflict without teacher intervention. He came away from the experience with new teaching insights, which he used to set up future learning experiences, such as the storyboarding session.

When teachers interpret documentation after a learning experience, they have the mental space to apprehend it in new ways. "Grappling with Greatness" began with an exchange between Thalia and Violet that their teacher, Joan, videotaped. Although physically present for the exchange, it wasn't until Joan reflected on it later that she wondered whether Violet's statement, "we all have different points of view," might prevent students from considering other perspectives more deeply. This subtle but significant difference became a focal point for Joan's inquiry over the ensuing months, leading to several moves, such as asking students to interview each other about the origins of their beliefs around human greatness.

Reflecting on documentation helps teachers gauge learners' current knowledge of a subject so they may teach in developmentally appropriate and differentiated ways. Documenting during moments when learners are demonstrating their knowledge can reveal thinking, understanding, and misconceptions that could otherwise be overlooked. In "The Yellow Door," when Nicole reviewed a video of Ava and Betel working together, she gained greater clarity of each girl's understanding of representing information through graphs. Although Betel seemed to get it by the end, Nicole resolved to find ways to build on Betel's developing awareness of the concept. Even more surprising to Nicole was her sense that, despite the difference in their abilities, both girls learned from this exchange. Although

Betel was more challenged by the content knowledge and learned more from Ava in this regard, Ava learned from Betel in the social realm through teaching her. Betel's self-assuredness and expressiveness provided Ava with immediate feedback on whether her communication strategies were getting through, enabling Ava to adjust her strategies until arriving at Betel's aha! moment. Also striking to Nicole was the two girls' perseverance. Nicole interpreted Ava's investment in representing her data correctly and Betel's willingness to listen and compromise as indications of how much the two cared about the work and their relationship. Nicole came away feeling the girls formed a good partnership and encouraged them to work together on subsequent occasions.

Interpreting Documentation with Colleagues Although teachers can deepen their understanding of their students by revisiting documentation on their own, it is even more beneficial to do it with others. Teaching can be an isolating profession. It is rare for teachers to visit each other's rooms while classes are in session or have the opportunity to share strategies with colleagues around specific teaching challenges. Documentation allows teachers to bring the eyes and ears of critical friends into their classroom and benefit from other perspectives.

Interpreting documentation from one's classroom with trusted peers is a powerful form of professional development for everyone involved, not just the teacher whose work is at the center of the conversation. Colleagues who know students from other contexts expand each other's knowledge of who students are and what engages them. Encountering other perspectives can expand, change, or strengthen teachers' impressions of learners, suggest ways to adapt curriculum, and generate fresh thinking around questions and strategies for moving learning forward.

Before the start of the kindergartners' study of the Boston Marathon, Ben and his colleagues developed an entry-point chart containing the various "hooks" the marathon might hold for each of the children based on previous experiences. For students like Christopher, who was generally interested in sports and competition, the connections were clear. For those less interested in sports, the teachers considered how to broaden the curriculum. For example, they decided to include stories of women's struggles to earn the right to run in the race because of one student's interest in a recent civil rights unit.

In "Grappling with Greatness," reflecting on documentation and associated questions with colleagues led Joan to rethink her goal of achieving consensus among students and provided new ideas for building students' listening skills and perspective-taking abilities. This story also revealed the benefit of a group of colleagues meeting over time: Joan and her colleagues had been meeting for more than five years with a focus on the overarching question, "How can deeper listening improve teaching and learning at our school?" The group helped Joan hold focus on this question and identify connections to her classroom.

Similarly, Amanda's inquiry in "Eyes on Engagement" resided within a larger context—a group of K–5 colleagues who met monthly to explore questions such as "How can we better understand and create the conditions for students to learn with and from each other?" and "How can we support and show our students as intellectual learners?" Despite the different ages and ability levels of their students, members of this group made connections between the teaching challenges and successes revealed in their colleagues' documentation and their own. From each session, teachers extracted ideas to try in their own classrooms. For example, a second grade teacher adapted Amanda's new "math menu" in choice time to give her students more choice and the option of doing fewer things in depth. Amanda's fourth grade colleague adopted Amanda's practice of videotaping and reflecting on group work with her students, and a kindergarten colleague was inspired by Amanda's work to try involving students in representing their learning on bulletin boards. Teachers documented what they tried and sought feedback at the next session. One teacher reported, "This feels different [from most professional development]. I like the problem-solving aspect of this. We don't get a chance to hear other suggestions for what to try very often. [Here] we learn about our own teaching instead of just being talked at. And we're looking at kids and kids' work . . . [which] gives you more of the kids' perspective."

Another benefit to forming cross-grade professional learning groups and grounding them in documentation is that teachers are better able to understand the developmental trajectory of learning and learners in their school. Seeing the knowledge, skills, and capacities learners need to succeed in later years helps teachers of younger students nurture the precursors to these skills in the early years. And teachers of older students come to appreciate the ways that teachers in the earlier grades lay the foundation for not only academic skills but also social and emotional learning as well.

Interpreting Documentation with Learners Although it may seem obvious to ask students about their learning and what helps or hinders it, many teachers overlook such questions. When teachers look at documentation with their students around epistemological questions, teachers and students can gain new insights that help inform future learning. Such reflective conversations grounded in documentation make the processes of learning visible to students. When teachers use these insights to inform instruction, and students use them to guide their activities and choices, the result is a classroom in which students feel empowered, represented, and engaged in purposeful learning.

Jill Hughes, a special needs teacher at the Wickliffe Progressive Community School in Ohio, began using documentation as a tool to help her students become better group learners. After discussing what a learning group looks like with her students, they decided to keep track of how often each student shared an idea, question, or suggestion during a group activity. One student suggested using colors to represent each person in the group and to put it in a bar graph with each bar representing a different activity so they could easily see each other's levels of participation (see figure 4). Every week, Jill had a thinking back conversation with each child to think about what factors contributed to his or her

Figure 4. Color-Coded Participation Chart

level of participation. One student who was often quiet realized she participated more in groups when she felt like others cared about what she did. She and Jill discussed what people could do to help her feel like she mattered, as well as how she could help others feel similarly. They decided to make a poster with speech bubbles to hang on the student's locker so she could refer to it before group activities. (See tool 16 in chapter 13 for more details about speech bubbles.) She titled it "Everyone counts." This kind of documentation gives learners a larger view on learning and who they are as learners, which they can bring to future learning experiences.

Documentation can capture the different viewpoints of students, enabling teachers and students to think about them in relation to each other. In the story about Lindy Johnson in chapter 8, Lindy was perplexed by the negativity of one group's response to her questions about learning from others during writers' workshop. Rather than coming to her own conclusions, Lindy shared the documentation and the questions it raised with her students. The subsequent conversation uncovered critical student perceptions about their own abilities and about Lindy's attitude toward them that negatively influenced the culture of the classroom. Making these perceptions visible allowed Lindy and her students to strategize together about what to change in order to move forward in a constructive way.

Moreover, by sharing the documentation and questions with her students and documenting their responses, Lindy made her own listening visible to them. Educators in Reggio Emilia often refer to documentation as "visible listening" because it creates the physical traces of listening and because the very act of documenting communicates to learners that teachers are listening. When teachers engage students in conversations about real questions and listen to and act on their responses, students feel empowered. At the end of the year, one student from Lindy's class approached her and said, "You're the only teacher I've ever had that listened to us when we have suggestions for the class." Similarly, several of Joan's students' comments at the end of the semester suggested that they noticed and appreciated that their opinions mattered to Joan. In Alex's words, ". . . there wasn't something [in particular] that you wanted here. You wanted my thinking . . ."

Reflecting with students after a learning experience allows teachers and students to engage in a kind of summative assessment together. Although not a replacement for tests, these conversations illuminate—for teachers and students—not only what but also how the group learned. At the end of "Grappling with Greatness," Joan and her students reflected on documentation—of themselves and of the adults' discussion. The students' comments provided evidence of content learning (in this case, their shifts in thinking about human greatness) and metacognition. Comments such as Owen's suggest that the students were aware that their thinking—about the topic and more generally—had changed and of the specific factors that led to that change:

> The topic got to mean more and more to us. But I was impressed by how far we went beyond greatness. We learned a lot more about the thinking process and about how to learn . . . how you sort of go about thinking about something . . . in this class, we had to know what we were thinking. But in a large class, it gets too easy to be quiet and too easy not to know what you think.

The students' insights into the learning process will be useful in future situations. Similarly, Joan developed a more nuanced understanding of the goal of reaching consensus, the role of listening in teaching and learning, and the value of choreographing learning experiences that capitalize on the intimacy of the small group as well as the diverse perspectives of the whole.

It is critical that teachers and students go through the process of interpreting—making meaning—before moving onto the next practice—sharing. The documentation we share should be selective—identified through the process of interpretation as having the potential to serve specific learning purposes for various audiences.

Sharing: Building Connections and Making Teaching and Learning Public

Sharing—the last of the four practices of documentation—is rooted in all five principles of learning discussed in chapter 7. Sharing documentation that makes learning and teaching visible reflects choices about what sorts of learning matters (purposeful); supports collective knowledge building (social); creates moments for taking pride in the work of students and teachers (emotional); shapes attitudes about who teachers and learners are and what they are capable of (empowering); and enables students and teachers to see themselves and their contributions reflected in the documentation itself (representational).

The matrix of documentation in four contexts introduced at the beginning of this chapter is particularly useful for considering why, when, and with whom to share documentation. The following strategies are grounded in the belief that sharing learning will lead to new learning for the learners themselves and for others. They are designed to create connections inside and outside the classroom and during and after the learning experience:

- Building collective knowledge within and across classrooms
- Engaging families through documentation
- Creating public exhibitions and products for a wider audience

Building Collective Knowledge Within and Across Classrooms Documentation supports the building of conceptual knowledge and collaboration across classrooms, grades, and subject matter. Making the thinking of all or other members of the learning group visible—and therefore accessible to one another—allows students to benefit from and build on what others know. It also helps a classroom become a learning community. Jennifer Hogue, a ninth grade English language arts teacher at Cambridge Rindge and Latin School who struggled to find documentation practices that felt authentic to her and her students, found a purpose for documentation after noticing that the quality of thinking students expressed in their writing was higher than in classroom discussions. Frustrated that she was the only one privy to her students' true capabilities, Jennifer began to share excerpts from student reflections and other writing in class, along with her own thinking and questions. Jennifer expanded on this practice over the course of the semester, eventually asking students (who were studying *Lord of the Flies*) to form study groups around the characters they found most compelling and to share their observations and questions on a character message board (see figure 5). These moves led the class to a deeper understanding of the characters' allegorical significance and the overarching themes the author was exploring.[7] By selectively bringing the group's attention to students' thinking, teachers enable the group to learn from the thinking of others, ultimately developing a more complex understanding of the subject matter.

Figure 5. *Lord of the Flies* **Character Message Board**

Keeping students' ideas and questions physically present in the classroom by posting quotes and speech bubbles helps connect student learning to what they are curious about and provides touchstones for the group to return to throughout a study (see tool 16 in chapter 13). Teachers identify moments to bring students' collective attention to these ideas and questions in order to harvest new thinking. In Elizabeth Glover's fifth grade classroom at Wickliffe, one student's observation, "The winner of a war writes the history of that war, so you never get to know or see the other side," and another's question, "Which document is more important, the Declaration of Independence or the Constitution?" were captured and posted in the classroom, along with other significant ideas and questions from students during a unit on early Americans. Elizabeth and her students returned to these quotes throughout the study as a way to deepen their thinking about key concepts in history, such as perspective and the importance of comparing multiple sources.

Making students' thinking public allows students to consider each other's approaches to learning as well, enabling them to learn from the strategies and even mistakes of their peers. In "The Yellow Door," the ideas and strategies of individuals became contagious when shared with the group. The initial idea to make more doors for the block area emerged from a conversation between Nicole and a small group of students. When Nicole shared the idea with the rest of the class, many enthusiastically joined in the project. Nicole continued to make students' thinking public throughout the project so ideas continued to spread. When the door design group saw Tamar's drawing—based on her precise measurements with a ruler—they were inspired to learn to measure. After Amelia shared her graph during morning meeting, other students adopted her strategy for organizing data.

In many schools, several classrooms study the same or related subjects concurrently. In elementary school, multiple classrooms at each grade level often follow the same curriculum. In middle and high schools, teachers often teach the same course to different groups of students several times a day. Yet seldom do these classrooms share students' work and learning outside the classroom while a study is underway to inform the learning of their peers.

"The Vernal Pool" illustrates what can happen when teachers and students join forces in this way. When the two seventh grade groups collaborated across classrooms, not only were students able to spend more time collectively at the pool but they also shared documentation and data across groups. This allowed students to make discoveries that might otherwise be overlooked—such as the rise in temperature during the day. In "The Amazing Circus Act," Joan and Nora's work was shaped by the questions of their peers who saw their work in the hallway. The question about whether eight feet of water was enough to successfully complete the stunt sent Joan and Nora on a quest for new answers, leading to new learning in physics.

Making learning visible outside the classroom also allows students to become teachers. In "The Yellow Door," seeing the fourth grade students' graphs prompted Nicole to use them to introduce her students to the concept of graphing information. Along with providing an accessible model that kindergartners can understand, the display motivated the kindergartners who were eager to do the same work as older students. Similarly, in "The Amazing Circus Act," Joan and Nora's hallway display motivated Neuza, the precalculus teacher, to invite the girls to present to her class as a way to lend relevance to her own students' studies. Taking the perspective of teacher and learner further solidified Joan and Nora's already substantial knowledge of the subject matter.

Engaging Families through Documentation Typically teachers share student work after it has become a product, whether it is a play, a painting, or a poem. What if teachers make the learning process visible to families and other care providers by making more of the processes and meaning behind what children are learning visible at various points during the learning experience? Sharing documentation provides a window into the classroom for students' families, deepening the connection between home and school and engaging parents as intellectual partners. Such documentation can enrich the conversations families have with their children about school, enhance the family's and teacher's understanding of how to support learning, and create new possibilities for parent participation in schools.

Just as documentation supports the reflection of teachers with students, it also supports parents' ability to have meaningful conversations with their children about school. Such documentation makes it possible to extend learning into the home in ways that range from asking more relevant questions to sharing parents' perspectives on a topic to assisting with projects. Gina Stefanini, a K–2 special needs teacher at the Devotion School in Brookline, Massachusetts, acquired a small fleet of inexpensive digital cameras that she sent home with students. The cameras contained photographs—some taken by her and other teachers but mostly taken by the students themselves. Photographs are effective visual prompts, especially for students who struggle with language, to share their school experiences and for parents to ask questions. Parents told Gina that conversations that previously consisted of posing a broad question and receiving a one-word response were becoming more specific and detailed. Students recalled more about their school experiences. Consider the following notes that parents took of their conversations and sent to Gina:

Parent–child conversation when not using digital images:

Parent: How was gym today?

Child: What?

Parent: You had gym today.

Child: Gym today?

Parent–child conversation when using digital images:

Parent: How was gym today?

Child: See me. I play at gym. I had the blue ball. I tag and Ann tags me. See, I run. I hit the red wall. I have gym today and Friday. Where is my ball? I want to play again.

Seeing Joan and Nora's documentation of their solution to the Ferris wheel problem in "The Amazing Circus Act" prompted Joan's father to talk about his own experience learning math. An engineer by trade, Joan's father had had to relearn the math he learned in high school when he went to college; he had forgotten it because he never truly understood it. He could see in Joan and Nora's work that they understood mathematical concepts in a way he hadn't. The conversations with her father strengthened Joan's own sense of the value and relevance of what she was learning.

Documentation shared with parents does not always have to feature their child in order to suggest ways to support learning at home. Sometimes, documentation is meant to be representative of children more broadly and contribute to collective knowledge about how children learn. When parents at the Wickliffe Progressive Community School were shown a video about the kindergartners' Boston Marathon project during a parent–teacher organization meeting, many reported coming away with new insights into their role in their child's learning. One parent, reflecting on a recent experience helping his kindergarten-aged daughter create a robot as part of a school project, wrote the following:

> I will turn the roles around. I will be the helper and focus more on letting the children figure things out for themselves, giving them support where needed . . . I began this robot experience . . . wanting to teach her new skills, and trying to help her to learn the "correct" way to do things. I have learned that through brainstorming together, putting my child in the driver's seat, documenting her thoughts and actions, and helping her to put them together as something concrete, I help to open her mind and learn to think—and in the process I can feel my mind is more open as well.[8]

Sharing documentation that makes teachers' strategies for supporting children's learning visible challenges parents' assumptions about how and what children can learn; it creates new possibilities for parents to interact with their children and the school. After the initial parent–teacher organization meeting at Wickliffe, Sabrina Walters, a Wickliffe teacher whose two children attend the school, helped form a parent study group. The group gathered monthly to share their own documentation and explore questions about supporting children's learning at home, such as "What is the importance of unstructured time for children's learning?" The group transformed annual school events such as Kindergarten 101 (an orientation to the school for prospective parents) and parent open houses by creating more of a focus on learning. Members of the group led small groups of parents in structured conversations based on documentation, encouraging a deeper analysis of what children were learning in school and how it connected to the questions and concerns of parents (see tool 17 in chapter 14). Furthermore, the group developed materials such as the "refrigerator reminder" (see tool 18 in chapter 14) to share with other parents what they were learning about children's learning and making it visible.

At Wickliffe, engaging families through documentation led some parents to become early advocates for the MLV work. These parents then took the lead in helping the school forge deeper connections with more families. Now, just as the documentation of the Boston Marathon study changed the beliefs and attitudes of Wickliffe parents about learning, documentation from the Wickliffe parent study group is influencing the attitudes and behaviors beyond their own community.

Creating Public Exhibitions and Products for a Wider Audience

Teachers who make learning and learners visible strive to connect what happens in school to the real world and make learning matter—to the learners and to the larger community. One way teachers do this is to engage learners in activities and projects they care about and to seek ways for student learning to culminate in shareable products, valued by members of the classroom, school, or wider community. Another is to create exhibitions of learning with students, colleagues, or other educators. There are many purposes and audiences for exhibitions and other public displays, including exhibitions of teacher learning that serve professional development purposes and schoolwide exhibitions that offer alternatives to prevailing accountability practices. We address the first type here and the second type in chapter 10.

The learning portraits reflect several instances of student learning resulting in products that serve a larger purpose than learning for learning's sake. This can be intentional from the beginning, such as in "The Yellow Door," when a problem or need was identified and became the impetus for the learning and teaching that followed. The idea for a product can also emerge along the way as teachers and learners come to recognize that what they are learning holds value for others. Whether intended from the start or conceived of at the end, creating meaningful products is a powerful form of the engaging group tasks discussed in chapter 8. The key is for teachers to develop greater sensitivity to opportunities for student learning to enter into the public sphere.

Learners come away from these experiences with a deeper sense of the value of learning and making positive contributions to their community. The kindergartners, who initially created the new doors for their own use in the block area, later spoke with pride about the fact that the next generation of kindergartners was using them. The students in "The Vernal Pool" were committed to "learning to do something to help [their] town." Audiences who encounter this work come away with a deeper appreciation of how young people think and what they can do.

Furthermore, when learners are encouraged to take ownership of creating public products and displays, the act of communicating their learning can lead to new insights and skills, and deeper connections throughout a school. Making learning visible in ways that are understandable and engaging to others requires learners to reflect, synthesize, and shape communication for a target audience. In "The Vernal Pool," students researched field guides as a genre and identified the strengths and shortcomings to keep in mind. They also identified markers of quality and carried out numerous cycles of revision to reach the standards they set for themselves. In "The Amazing Circus Act," Joan and Nora tried to take the perspective of their intended audience (other high school students outside the interactive mathematics program). Their goal—to reduce the complexity of the equation— led to innovative communication techniques, such as using different colors and patterns to break the equation into conceptual chunks. Their teacher, Doug, thought this idea reflected the girls' ability to do high-level abstracting, one of the biggest accomplishments in mathematics. The girls' display also reflects their understanding of the need to appeal to the viewer's emotions by communicating a sense of drama in their title and problem statement.

Creating public exhibitions is a way to build the field of education by making visible what good teaching and learning looks like. Exhibitions that focus on innovative and high-quality teaching and learning allow other teachers to see what is possible and build their capacity to teach. Exhibitions are particularly effective in inspiring teachers to experiment with new strategies when they reflect the contexts and address the challenges of the teachers who view them. Several of the learning portraits in this book began as exhibits in such exhibitions. "The Yellow Door" was one of ten exhibits by Boston public school early childhood teachers in an exhibition at Wheelock College.[9] The purpose of the exhibition was to share ways that teachers can attend to standards by capitalizing on children's interests rather than strictly adhering to prescribed curriculum. "The Yellow Door" was joined by nine other exhibits that included stories such as one child's interest in playing baseball at recess turning into a lesson in problem solving and numeracy for the whole class and another child's impulse to teach peers to make paper airplanes turning into a larger project about sharing expertise by making how-to books (see figure 6).

Exhibitions of teacher work are equally powerful when they provide forums for teacher inquiry that extend beyond a close group of colleagues and engage a wider audience of educators in conversations about teaching. Joan Soble, Doug McGlathery, Jennifer Hogue, and several dozen of their colleagues over the years have mounted seven annual exhibitions at Cambridge Rindge and Latin School in which they have made their questions, challenges, successes, and even failures public. Although these exhibitions represent a great deal of extra work for teachers, and the act of exposing their teaching can feel risky, the rewards are many. For Doug, it is an opportunity to communicate and garner support for more interactive and authentic ways of approaching math instruction. For Joan, it is an opportunity to demonstrate that teaching for understanding and the rigor of AP courses are not mutually exclusive. For their colleague Debi Milligan, a photography teacher who has participated in all six of the high school exhibitions, it is an opportunity to hone in on a question about teaching and learning and to "examine it, document it, and come away at the end of the year [with] new understandings of my students, my teaching, my colleagues,

Can You Teach Me to Make a Paper Airplane?

This documentation highlights just a few moments during a nine-month project about flight. Our school is just a mile away from Logan International Airport. From our playground, we watch the planes take off over the harbor and fly over the cityscape. During rare quiet moments, we can hear the jet engines roar overhead, so it wasn't a surprise when the children in my class started to show an interest in flight.

One morning during choice time, Bella decided to construct an airplane of paper towel tubes. She experimented with different types of glue and tape until she had a sturdy shape. She spent the next several days painting and adding details. Other children became inspired by Bella's work; they wanted to build airplanes, too. When they asked me how, I directed them to Bella. Bella taught a few children, and then they taught more children. Pretty soon most of the twenty-two four year olds had built a paper towel tube airplane!

The children began to build airplanes with more materials: unit blocks, unfix cubes, and magnatiles. Their drawings of airplanes became more and more sophisticated as they poured through books about airplanes and closely examined photographs.

One day I took aside a small group of children who seemed particularly interested in flight and asked if anyone knew how to make a paper airplane. The children spent several minutes folding and manipulating the paper. Two girls knew just how to make a paper airplane. They taught the others, through words and demonstration, step by step, how to make a paper airplane. I helped the children who were struggling to fold the paper. Soon the children had their own paper airplanes. We took them into the hallway and let them fly!

Over the weeks we experimented with different paper airplane designs, discovering which ones flew the farthest. The children in the original group were becoming quite adept at making paper airplanes!

One morning, during the children's choice time, I noticed an interesting drawing, abandoned on the art table. I recognized the handwriting immediately.

Ms Frazier: *Samky, tell me about your drawing?*

Samky: *I made it for Sarah to show her the steps how to make a paper airplane.*

Throughout that morning, I noticed Samky teaching other children how to make a paper airplane.

I thought about how to capitalize on Samky's brilliant representation of folding a paper airplane. The following day I asked her if she could help me make a book to keep in the art studio. A *How-to Book*, that could teach children to make a paper airplane. Samky carefully redrew pictures of each step. Then she dictated the directions. Samky's drawings and words, alongside a photograph of her work, are displayed in the following panels.

Figure 6. Initial Panel of a "How-to Exhibit"

and myself as a creative contributor to this eclectic [school] community . . . If I didn't participate in this work, it would just be another year gone by."

For all of these teachers, contributing to the exhibitions of teaching and learning helps them articulate and clarify the values and principles that got them into teaching in the first place. In chapter 10, we will describe yet another kind of exhibition that attempts to provide an alternative form of accountability.

Chapter 10
Making Learning Visible in an Age of Accountability

Lois Hetland, a Project Zero colleague, was once visiting a public elementary school when she noticed the frequency of numbered standards and their descriptions displayed in classrooms and hallways (e.g., "Math Standard 5.NBT.5: Fluently multiplies multi-digit whole numbers using the standard algorithm"). Lois wondered what sense students made of all these standards so she stopped a student passing by and asked if she knew what standards were. The student replied, "I don't know but they're everywhere!"

Standards and accountability are indeed everywhere in our current political and educational climate. The trend toward ever-more accountability measures and outsourcing the evaluation of learning to external evaluators suggests a fundamental lack of trust in teachers. Soon after teachers first encounter the ideas and practices presented in this book, they often express feelings of frustration, dismay, and concern at the limited time or space to make learning and learners visible. Not only are teachers under pressure for students to score well on state and national tests but also many teachers increasingly face the threat of having their pay, and even their jobs, tied to student performance on these tests. The question we have heard more than any other is "How can I take the time to document and support learning in groups when I am expected to teach to the standards and am held accountable if my students perform poorly on individually administered tests?"

In this chapter, we address this question head on. We describe how teachers featured in this book and others working in public school classrooms subject to the pressures of high-stakes testing have made learning and learners visible. We then address how standards and the practices of group learning and documentation can work together and suggest an alternative way to think about accountability in and outside the classroom and school.

Three Examples of Supporting Standards-based Practice

What does it look like when teachers work with standards in ways that make learning and learners visible? The learning portraits described in the beginning of this book paint a complex picture of the teaching and learning process. They reveal teachers making purposeful choices about what is learned, designing the learning process in ways that engage and empower students, and collecting a variety of evidence of individual and group learning. We return to three of the teachers from the learning portraits—Nicole Chasse of "The Yellow Door," Amanda Van Vleck of "Eyes on Engagement," and Joan Soble of "Grappling with Greatness"—to examine how public school teachers at the primary, elementary, and high school levels use group learning and documentation to hold themselves accountable to district and state standards.

Nicole Chasse of "The Yellow Door"

Asking children to work in small groups, whether in the arts, math, social studies, or any other subject, is at the core of Nicole's teaching strategies for meeting standards. She frequently forms small groups based on children's interests, enlisting parent volunteers to help facilitate them. Rather than starting her lesson planning with standards, Nicole often begins planning with children's interests in mind. As a result, Nicole believes children exhibit greater ownership of their learning.

Nicole also groups together children with complementary skills so they can support each other on different aspects of the task. Then, even when children work on individual assignments, they can draw on each other for support, whether in spelling, coming up with a story idea, or comparing observational drawings. In general, Nicole observes with an eye toward particularly useful strategies or stubborn problems that children can bring to the large group—ideally accompanied by documentation such as a photograph, a verbal exchange, or children's work. Nicole intentionally makes the children's areas of expertise visible so they will look to each other for help. The large group serves as a valued source of feedback on making plans, selecting materials, problem solving, and more.

The door study emerged from a major conflict that led to a great deal of negative behavior. At first, Nicole had no idea how the project would connect to standards; her primary goal was to maintain a positive classroom climate in as constructive a way as possible by seeking student input on a solution they were likely to own. However, once the social dilemma was resolved, Nicole saw other learning opportunities in the children's interest in doors, leading her to embed the math standards of collecting, categorizing, and graphing information in the project.

A central purpose of the Massachusetts history and social science standards is to prepare students to participate fully in a democratic society. Although Nicole had already begun to teach a unit on attributes using math manipulatives, she decided to change course and send children to investigate different parts of the school building armed with a meaningful goal. Exploring the school's public spaces helped children feel they were members of a larger community of learners. They saw that learning did not occur just in their classroom or just in the kindergarten wing—opportunities to learn extended well beyond those settings. The classroom became a place to which children could return, discuss their discoveries, and then venture out again. The sight of kindergartners with clipboards led other students and teachers to inquire about their task; communicating the rationale behind their activities further deepened the children's understanding.

Nicole also enlisted school colleagues to help her students meet the standards. During the door study, she consulted the math specialist to incorporate specific math standards such as comparing and classifying measurable attributes of objects into the children's work. Nicole and Gretchen Albertini (a third grade teacher whose students were buddies with Nicole's class) used the students' partnerships to support the learning expectations for each class. During a unit about the ocean, the kindergartners formed interest-based groups to research a sea creature and create a work of art and informational book to present to their third grade buddies. The buddies, in turn, interviewed the kindergartners before their presentations, took notes during the talks, and wrote letters to the younger children afterward, articulating what they had learned. In another unit, the kindergartners used tally marks to collect and record data on the number of insects and anthills they found on the playground. Nicole asked them to explain their task to their older buddies, in part as a form of assessment. The buddies also helped the younger children add up the tallies when the numbers became too big for them to track.

Such shared investment in a task motivates children to collaborate and engage in purposeful debate so they come to school not just to learn content but also eager to work with their group. During year-end reflections, children often choose collaborative projects such as the door study as one of their most rewarding accomplishments.

Amanda Van Vleck of "Eyes on Engagement"

Amanda's initial interest in MLV stemmed from a desire to find evidence of learning to complement—and sometimes challenge—results from standardized tests. For example, one student, who rarely demonstrated self-monitoring in any subject area and consistently failed standardized tests as a result, showed she was able to reflect on and correct a mistake during a classroom math lesson. Because standardized tests typically require only the final answer, they provide no insight into the process a learner goes through to reach an answer.

Amanda often observes learning in her classroom that would never be recognized on state tests, no matter how thoughtfully designed. Such learning usually occurs when students are working in small groups. Amanda has found that if she is present for students' conversations, the path from naive awareness to sophisticated understandings is actually mappable. Amanda notes the following:

> Those observed pathways were helpful to me as I figured out ways to draw more students onto a path of understanding, but they also were helpful to other students who got to see the progression from confusion to clarity. Capturing and sharing aha! moments in math with PowerPoints is an example of a journey to understanding that I needed all students to understand. Had I left that moment undocumented, many students would have missed key concepts about categorizing numbers.

Over time, Amanda draws more and more on documentation and group learning to help students meet state standards. For example, the Massachusetts English language arts curriculum framework includes the following standard for reading literature: "Refer to details and examples in a text when explaining what the text says explicitly and when drawing inferences from the text." At the beginning of each year, Amanda shares a number of interactive read-alouds that she will use later on to model text structures or writing styles that are part of state standards. When her class read *The Other Side* by Jacqueline Woodson, a story about a pair of young girls trying to make sense of segregation in a rural, southern neighborhood, several students wondered about the girls' ages. Although the age of the characters was not critical to understanding the story's message, the students became highly invested in determining whether or not the characters were peers. Students made comments such as the following:

"Did you see the toys in Clover's house? Those are younger toys. She must be a little kid."

"Yeah, but her mom lets her go outside by herself. She can't be too young."

"She mentioned something about school so she is definitely kindergarten or older."

Although Amanda was not targeting the skill of text-based inference at the time, she documented the conversation so it could be revisited later in the year when she was planning to teach inference. When she shared this documentation with students to illustrate inference in action (their action), seeing their peers and themselves using these strategies on their own had a much bigger impact than a more generalized example would have. Especially for students who are often not listened to or respected, documentation signals that what they say and do matters. Amanda comments,

> This work . . . reminds me to be quiet and let learners speak and question and problem-solve . . . Documentation sheds light not just on the learning of learners, but also on the teaching moments that are captured and missed . . . it allows my students to be learners at all times [and] to be experts at things not measured by traditional tests.

When students ask Amanda why the cameras are always out and she is constantly taking notes, she responds she doesn't want to miss their stories, words, ideas, or confusions (see figure 7 for Amanda's occasions for documentation). Amanda and her students are partners in teaching and learning—all learning with and from others.

Joan Soble of "Grappling with Greatness"

In her teaching of the AP English course, Joan feels accountable for her students' performance on the AP exam—an individually administered high-stakes test. Yet in

---

Amanda's Occasions for Documentation

When Do I Document?

- When my absence from the learning experience will not adversely affect the learning
- When I notice a pattern in behavior, confusion, or ideas that I want others to notice
- When I or an individual or group of students is struggling or has a question and wants to understand someone or something more completely
- When I want to tell or help a child to tell a story of learning
- When an "Aha!" moment seems to be happening for an individual or group
- When we are working on a specific skill, strategy, or routine, and need evidence to assess progress
- When I know someone will ask, "What are they learning from doing this?"
- When I anticipate changes in thinking, understanding, or behaving over time
- When I find myself feeling like things *are* or *are not* "going well" and I need evidence to support my perception
- When I sense a quality of engagement or disengagement that is striking
- When groups (small or large, successful or unsuccessful) are working together without teacher facilitation
- When I notice purposeful and connected discourse of almost any kind
- When language or memory is a weakness for one or more students
- Sometimes, *after* the experience (notes can be jotted down from memory or photos reenacted) to travel back in time and facilitate revisiting

Figure 7. Amanda Van Vleck's Occasions for Documentation

preparing students to take the exam, Joan draws as much as possible on the power of the group to inform students' understanding of literature and good writing and develop their own points of view. Especially with the most challenging literature, students often need each other to even begin to tackle it. In keeping with the Common Core State Standards' emphasis on collaboration, Joan's efforts have expanded her students' thinking about themes in literature and deepened their understanding of the value of listening and the purposes of learning together.

One tool Joan uses to support such learning is VoiceThread—a web-based application that enables participants to have asynchronous conversations around collections of images, videos, and documents. VoiceThread is a useful tool for documentation because it elicits student voices and preserves them as a reference for future learning. Participants can then leave comments using voice, text, or video. At the beginning of the semester, few students saw the significance of listening to their peers as a way to develop their own understanding. Over time, documenting student learning not only allowed Joan to see what her students were learning but also gave students the opportunity to learn from each other. This, in turn, opens up a space for a different kind of learning. In her final reflection, one student wrote,

> To my surprise, I found that my peers' comments [on *The Love Song of J. Alfred Prufrock*] served as a gateway to my own understanding of the poem. Reading an analysis of a stanza that one individual posted, and comparing it to the analysis offered by another, kick-started my own thoughts about the meaning of a given line, and allowed me to fill in my own gaps of understanding with interpretations offered by others.

Another student reflected,

> I thought that teachers were the only ones wise enough and qualified enough to teach their students. However, after my conversation with Maria, where I was taught a very important lesson by a fellow classmate, I realized that students can actually teach students and am now fully prepared for school activities where students work together and teach each other.

Veteran teachers such as Joan make a distinction between the big ideas behind the standards and the individual standards that tend to treat knowledge as discrete facts. They strike a balance between designing their curriculum to address essential concepts in their disciplines and preparing their students to succeed on standardized tests, often through explicit "test prep." Standards are also useful at the department level for identifying what is most important to teach at different grade levels and which topics might be overlooked in the current curriculum. Although newer teachers often find standards helpful as a guide to the goals and markers they need to reach, they also find MLV practices useful in deciding how to get there.

MLV invites more kinds of learning into the room and slows down teachers so they get to know their students better. Beyond the AP test, Joan feels accountable for the full spectrum of student learning, including the so-called twenty-first-century skills—

communication, creativity, collaboration, and critical thinking. Conversations with colleagues that are grounded in documentation of student learning provide an alternative methodology for determining when such learning has taken place. In "Grappling with Greatness," videos of student conversations helped Joan and her colleagues assess her students' discourse skills. Students were also able to reflect on the role of the group in furthering their learning. As one student commented, "I have discovered that often the most significant learning experiences have happened in class when I and other students are able to share ideas and build on each other's opinions."

Ways MLV Practices and Standards Work Together

The strategies used by Nicole, Amanda, and Joan are efforts to identify critical benchmarks for what counts as meaningful learning in an intellectual community. Their choices mirror other thoughtful attempts (such as the Common Core State Standards and the Partnership for 21st Century Skills) to reframe the learning of basic content within larger skills and dispositions such as curiosity, critical thinking, and collaboration. Addressing and clarifying conceptions of what is most important to learn with parents, teachers, students, administrators, and school boards are crucial conversations to have about any educational endeavor. Looking across the practices employed by Nicole, Amanda, Joan, and other teachers using MLV ideas and practices suggests at least three ways that making learning and learners visible can help teachers address standards.

Bridging Students and Standards

Many people equate standards with standardization or standardized tests, but in fact standards do allow for variation in how teachers teach and students demonstrate understanding. As the authors of the Common Core make clear, standards "do not dictate curriculum or teaching methods."[1] Conflating standards with standardized tests undercuts the critical role of standards in identifying essential knowledge and skills that learners need to function effectively in the world. Teachers who make learning and learners visible seek to bridge the standards on the page to the diversity of learners in their classrooms. Documentation is key to helping teachers connect the curriculum to the learners in front of them.

In planning the activity centered on "The Vernal Pool," teachers Mandy Locke and Matt Leaf drew on curriculum maps created by teachers and administrators at the Four Rivers Charter Public School. These maps charted learning goals for students at each grade level based on state standards and school values. As the curriculum unfolded, Mandy and Matt were alert to student interests that might connect to standards. For example, student musings about why the pool doesn't fill up with leaves provided an entry point into food chains. The teachers also translated their learning goals into student-friendly language. For example, the writing standards of "Ideas are supported with explanation and detail . . ." and "The writing exhibits craftsmanship through correct use of English conventions" became "I can write a field guide that is informative and interesting."

Over the course of the year, Mandy and Matt worked to ensure that all of the seventh grade learning goals were met. For the vernal pool project, they created experiences that addressed a wide range of science, English language arts (e.g., creating folk tales), math (e.g., ratio and proportions used to make the guidebook drawings), visual arts, health, and wellness (e.g., safety in fieldwork), and character goals (e.g., group collaboration). See figure 8 for Massachusetts standards in science and ELA addressed in the vernal pool project.

Grounding Standards in a Shared Reference Point

The translation of standards into practice is seldom straightforward. What one person considers a demonstration of understanding may not look the same as another's. Although most people would likely agree that the standards named in figure 8 are important for seventh-graders to master, describing what each standard looks like in operation is much more difficult. Consider English language arts standard 21.6: "Revise writing to improve organization and diction after checking the logic underlying the order of ideas, the precision of vocabulary used, and the economy of writing." What does this look like in practice? The documentation collected by Mandy and Matt—the drafts and final versions of students' writing, the recordings of peer feedback sessions, and the learning portrait itself—create a shared reference point for determining whether different standards are met. Such documentation also enables the students to learn from what their peers think.

Collaborative review of documentation grounds adult conversations about standards in actual artifacts of student learning that can be used to support or challenge an interpretation; it also allows for multiple perspectives. Joan Soble and her colleagues used documentation to develop a shared language and vision of what different standards of teaching and learning look like in various disciplines. Questions such as "How can we improve student discourse at our school?" provide a focus for the collection and analysis of documentation. Similarly, when administrators ground observations of teachers' practice in documentation, formerly evaluative conversations become more focused on the learning of students and teachers.

Many of the capacities and dispositions identified in the standards are not achieved in a lesson, a unit, or even a year; rather, they are developed over time. Yet most teachers have a year or less with their students. Collective review of documentation allows for cross-grade conversations about whether and when standards are being reached. In Amanda Van Vleck's school, kindergarten through fourth grade teachers met regularly to look at classroom videotape to examine how learning in groups can be nurtured over time. At Cambridge Rindge and Latin School, twelfth grade teachers created exhibits to explore the learning successes and challenges around the pilot of a new senior project. Administrators and teachers from different grades used the exhibits to ground a conversation about "lessons learned." One outcome of this conversation was the identification of experiences and skills best introduced in the ninth grade and built on throughout the following years.

Demonstrating Other Kinds of Learning

When standardized tests are the sole or primary measure of whether students have learned, there is little to no allowance for variation in how students demonstrate

Table 1: Massachusetts State Science and English Language Arts Standards	
Earth Science	1. Recognize, interpret, and be able to create models of the earth's common physical features in various mapping representations, including contour maps.
	3.4 Explain how water flows into and through a watershed. Explain the roles of aquifers, wells, porosity, permeability, water table, and runoff.
	3.5 Describe the processes of the hydrologic cycle, including evaporation, condensation, precipitation, surface runoff and groundwater percolation, infiltration, and transpiration.
Biological Science	1. Classify organisms into the currently recognized kingdoms according to characteristics that they share. Be familiar with organisms from each kingdom.
	13. Give examples of ways in which organisms interact and have different functions within an ecosystem that enable the ecosystem to survive.
	14. Explain the roles and relationships among producers, consumers, and decomposers in the process of energy transfer in a food web.
	16. Recognize that producers (plants that contain chlorophyll) use the energy from sunlight to make sugars from carbon dioxide and water through a process called photosynthesis. This food can be used immediately, stored for later use, or used by other organisms.
English Language Arts	19.19 Write stories or scripts with well-developed characters, setting, dialogue, clear conflict and resolution, and sufficient descriptive detail.
	19.22 Write and justify a personal interpretation of literary, informational, or expository reading that includes a topic statement, supporting details from literature, and a conclusion.
	19.23 Write multi-paragraph compositions that have clear topic development, logical organization, effective use of detail, and variety in sentence structure.
	20.4 Select and use appropriate rhetorical techniques for a variety of purposes, such as to convince or entertain the reader.
	21.6 Revise writing to improve organization and diction after checking the logic underlying the order of ideas, the precision of vocabulary used, and the economy of writing.
	21.7 Improve word choice by using a variety of references.
	22.8 Use knowledge of types of sentences (simple, compound, complex), correct mechanics (comma after introductory structures), correct usage (pronoun reference), sentence structure (complete sentences, properly placed modifiers), and standard English Spelling when writing and editing.
	23.10 Organize information into a coherent essay or report with a thesis statement in the introduction, transition sentences to link paragraphs, and a conclusion.
	24.4 Apply steps for obtaining information from a variety of sources, organizing information, documenting sources, and presenting research in individual projects: • differentiate between primary and secondary source materials; • differentiate between paraphrasing and using direct quotes in a report; • organize and present research using the grade 7–8 Learning Standards in the Composition Strand as a guide for writing; • document information and quotations and use a consistent format for footnotes or endnotes; and • use standard bibliographic format to document sources.
	25.4 As a group, develop and use scoring guides or rubrics to improve organization and presentation of written and oral projects.

Figure 8. Massachusetts State Science and ELA Standards[2]

understanding. Yet standardized tests rarely, if ever, capture capacities such as collaboration, imagination, or empathy. Practices such as documentation provide evidence of student learning for educators who question the primacy of standardized tests as the only meaningful indicator of what students have learned.

Moreover, although test scores reflect individual achievement, they have little or nothing to say about the processes and contexts of learning for individuals or groups. Documentation enables greater awareness of the factors that influence students' individual and group learning and generates hypotheses about how teachers can best support that learning. The documentation and group learning practices shared in this book honor and enhance the quality of children's learning in the here and now, not just as preparation for a future goal or outcome.

Reggio educators challenge the assertion that learning is a process that can be verified only after the fact as a kind of post mortem. If the adage "what we measure is what we value" is accurate, then our assessments need to show the learning processes as well as learning products. The learning portraits in this book and the extraordinary visual essays and documentation panels created by Reggio educators are just such a demonstration of children's learning in the very process of creating, thinking, and knowing.[3]

The learning portraits reveal learning and learners in action. In "The Yellow Door," one can see Ava and Betel expanding their knowledge of graphing along with a deepening of respect for one another. In "Grappling with Greatness," Liam, Violet, and their classmates deepened their understanding about what makes a person great along with learning about thinking. In "Meet the Directors," Simon developed a sense of the need to put things in order as well as the value of feedback in learning. In all these examples, documentation of the learning process provides evidence of learning that complements the learning products.

Three Realms of Accountability

Quantification of progress is but one way to share evidence of learning and achievement, yet it comes at a high cost if it is the only way to judge powerful learning. As the social scientist Donald Campbell points out, "The more any quantitative social indicator is used for social decision making, the more subject it will be to corruption pressures and the more apt it will be to distort and corrupt the social processes it is intended to monitor."[4] One need look no further than the many unintended outcomes of the high-stakes testing movement—the nationwide reports of cheating by teachers and administrators, the temptation to keep low-scoring students from taking tests, the narrowing of curriculum, the dedication of precious class time to test preparation, and the high rate of teachers leaving the profession—to recognize the prescience of Campbell's observation.[5] This book makes the case that qualitative forms of sharing evidence—via learning portraits, student work, photographs, quotes, and video—are powerful ways to shift the dialogue among stakeholders to a fuller view of what counts as learning.

Documentation introduces another form of data into the school culture—tangible artifacts of the learning and teaching process. These artifacts possess a certain amount of face validity; they also suggest another way in which members of a learning community can be accountable to themselves and to others. Here we put forth an alternative view of accountability in three realms—to oneself, to members of a learning community, and to the larger community; documentation plays a central role in each realm.[6]

Accountability to Self

Teachers become accountable to themselves and their students when they become students of their own teaching. Our colleague Steve Seidel[7] describes this type of accountability as philosophical as opposed to psychometric justification. Seidel suggests that, in the United States, we are so enamored of psychometric and "scientific" accountability that we seem to have forgotten there could be any other kind. Accountability to oneself entails being thoughtful about what is worth learning and teaching, collecting documentation to determine the impact of what is taught, and using that information to inform future learning.

Somewhat paradoxically, being accountable to oneself often entails seeking out others so as not to rely on one's own subjective view and not to avoid the hard questions. In "Grappling with Greatness," Joan and her colleagues reflected on documentation of class discussions to determine whether students were thoughtfully considering other students' perspectives. Debi Milligan, a photography teacher and colleague of Joan's, explains philosophical justification in her teaching and collaboration with colleagues as follows: "Making learning visible keeps your eye on the ball to think together about what you're doing. You could get distracted very easily by things that are very trivial that don't really matter. Questions such as 'why do you do this work' force you into answering in a way that helps you clarify the principles you are holding and want to keep track of."

Unlike standardized test scores, documentation helps teachers learn about their teaching and its impact at a time when they can use that information to enhance future learning. By making learning and learners visible, documentation helps teachers stay close to students' understandings, misconceptions, and interests. As mentioned in chapter 9, viewing video documentation of the day's lesson reminded Ben Mardell of his students' interest in the length of the marathon and whether they would be able to run 26.2 miles. Ben used that information to plan the next day's lesson. Lin Tucker, a science specialist and colleague of Amanda Van Vleck, notes the following:

> Documentation and attending to the group provide "reality" checks for the teacher. It's all too easy to "teach" something and believe students have "learned" it—a static process. Documentation and trusting that students learn effectively in peer interaction (for various reasons from having to verbalize ideas and entertain different points of view to feeling more engaged and in charge) reveal the organic nature of learning and provide the information a teacher needs to maximize the learning of the students. The teacher actively learns while teaching and, in doing so, models the power of documentation and evidence to modify strategy and effect change rather than judge and punish.

Accountability to Each Other

Members of a school community become accountable to each other when they take responsibility for contributing to the learning of others as well as their own and form a collective identity as a community that learns. Making learning and learners visible plays a key role in fostering this sense of individual and group commitment in the classroom and the staffroom.

Through close examination of learning moments in the classroom, teachers expand their understanding of students' capabilities, including their ability to learn from each other. Rather than directing the learning themselves or constantly providing answers, teachers refer students to each other. Teachers often ask students to think about what might be important for others to know about what they are learning. In "The Amazing Circus Act," Joan and Nora's initial impulse to create a hallway display that celebrated their work was soon superseded by their focus on the learning experience of the viewer. Joan and Nora wanted other students to understand the mathematical formula as well as they did—hence they assessed their work based on how well they engaged and communicated with a less knowledgeable audience. Bringing attention to sharing learning with others—whether before, during, or after a learning experience—fosters metacognition and often leads to greater clarity and understanding.

Along with changing expectations around the focus and purpose of hallway displays, accountability for each other's learning influences such school structures as staff meetings and teacher evaluations. Most of the teachers in the learning portraits belong to study groups in which members regularly share documentation as a way to deepen their own and their colleagues' understanding of how children learn. They regularly invite colleagues and parents into their classrooms—literally as well as through documentation—to seek other perspectives and for instructional support. Nicole and Ben ask parents to help document classroom projects and share relevant expertise. Teacher evaluations also become more grounded in documentation of student learning, with teachers and administrators contributing their perspectives.

Classrooms studying related topics also offer opportunities to contribute to collective knowledge. In "The Vernal Pool," the two seventh grade sections shared notes on the aquatic life they observed, comparing similarities and differences en route to building and testing their theories. In "The Yellow Door," Nicole invited her kindergartners to see the work of a fourth grade class in order to spark ideas about how they might organize and share their data. The kindergartners also left the doors they created as a gift for future classes.

Accountability to the Larger Community

Exhibitions of student and teacher learning offer schools another way to be accountable to the broader community. When teachers share evidence of valued student learning not typically reflected on standardized tests to varied constituents, it opens up a dialogue around educational values and schooling. The Wickliffe Progressive Community School in Ohio held its first schoolwide exhibition in spring 2007 as a way to explore alternative forms of accountability. In the words of Wickliffe's former principal, Fred Burton,

> Testing and accountability aren't always artfully done, but it's not enough just to say that without trying to create some alternatives . . . to be more accountable to ourselves, to each other, and to the community. These exhibits are another way to see children and the kind of intellectual life that children and teachers have at Wickliffe.[8]

Although standardized test scores provide some insight into whether teachers and schools are successfully teaching basic skills and content knowledge, rarely do they illuminate other qualities of the school experience or important learning beyond the scope of the test. Nor do they provide timely and useful insights into teaching or fulfilling a school's mission more effectively. The need for documentation as an alternative form of assessment is grounded in the principles of learning introduced in chapter 7—the belief that much of what constitutes learning cannot always be reached, expressed, or captured through oral or written language, much less predetermined curriculum or standardized tests.

Knowing their learning extends beyond school walls lends authenticity to students' learning. For students in "The Vernal Pool," awareness that their work had real implications for protecting a natural resource in their community motivated them to forgo breaks and stay after school. Wickliffe's exhibitions of learning processes and products expand the community's image of children's intellectual, emotional, and aesthetic capabilities. Ben Mardell's documentation of the Boston Marathon not only informed next steps in the study but also demonstrated to other educators and parents the enormous potential of young children and the power of the group as a context for learning.

Making learning visible through the products students create, exhibitions, learning portraits, and other public forums is an opportunity to bring attention to the particular learning experiences and educational approaches valued by an institution and its members. Such documentation allows projects to be shared outside their original context as a way to provoke assumptions, values, and beliefs about how and what children learn. Sharing documentation with this intention can be seen as a political act—a way to shape public perception of young people, the purpose of schooling, and educational policies.

The psychologist Lev Vygotsky said that "children grow into the intellectual life of those around them."[9] The goal of the practices described in this book is to create intellectual communities where children and adults alike develop their ideas and their identities as learners. These learning communities engage students and teachers as active and reflective participants, making the purposeful, social, representational, empowering, and emotional principles of learning visible.

We recognize that making learning and learners visible is complex and time-consuming work, and are saddened by the reality that far too many teachers face organizational constraints that make some of these practices feel out of reach. At the same time, in the words of our Reggio Emilia colleagues, making learning visible makes learning possible. We take courage from and find inspiration in the work of educators in Reggio Emilia and the United States (many of whom are featured in this book) who, with their students, create an environment in which individual and group learning are able to thrive. For them, making learning and learners visible is not additional work; it *is* the work.

PART III: Tools for Making Learning and Learners Visible

This section provides resources and tools to support the practices of group learning and documentation discussed in the rest of this book. Many of the tools are distillations of the ways teachers have applied MLV ideas and practices about group learning and documentation in their classrooms. Some resources are directed toward teachers, some toward administrators, and others toward families and community members. Most entail a careful review of student thinking and learning in order to deepen understanding about teaching and learning. There is no exact recipe for making learning visible and it will take time to identify and adapt the tools and resources for your own setting. The following chapters comprise five categories of tools and resources:

- Supporting learning in groups in the classroom
- Supporting learning in groups in the staffroom
- Documenting individual and group learning
- Engaging families in supporting student learning
- Making learning visible beyond the classroom

Almost every tool can be adapted for classrooms from preschool through high school. All five chapters include tools that are relevant for teachers. "Supporting Learning in Groups in the Staffroom" and "Making Learning Visible beyond the Classroom" are especially relevant for administrators. "Engaging Families in Supporting Student Learning" is useful for families.

Chapter 11
Supporting Learning in Groups in the Classroom

This chapter includes practical tools that teachers can use to create learning groups throughout the school year and promote a culture of dialogue.

Tool 1. Getting Started with Making Learning Visible
This tool provides a useful introduction to practices of documentation and group learning for adults new to these ideas—new teachers, paraprofessionals, student teachers, and others. We identify five concrete ways to create a community of learners such as the use of documentation to promote collaboration and strategies for developing learners' capacity for peer feedback.

Tool 2. Looking at Learning in Groups: Classroom Discussion Guidelines
This tool offers an engaging way to launch conversations with students about how learning groups form, function, and demonstrate understanding. It includes questions such as "What are some things you learn best by yourself?" "What are some things you learn best in a group?" and "How do you decide on things in a group?"

Tool 3. Considerations for Forming Small Groups
Here, we identify eight factors to keep in mind when forming small groups: size, stability, gender, cultural background, students' interests, competencies, friendship, and student input.

Tool 4. Entry-Point Charts: Engaging All Members of the Group
This tool provides a structure to help teachers ensure that all learners are engaged in the learning. Whereas many teachers think about how to engage students informally, entry-point charts enable teachers to record these thoughts so they can be revised and shared.

Tool 5. Structures for Giving and Receiving Feedback
Last, we describe different structures for supporting students in learning from and with each other. Giving and receiving feedback from peers encourages learners to see themselves as sources of knowledge and consider multiple perspectives.

1 GETTING STARTED WITH MAKING LEARNING VISIBLE

No matter where, what, or who you teach, creating a learning community is essential to your students' learning. Teachers new to MLV ideas sometimes wonder how to begin. This tool provides a quick introduction to group learning and documentation practices that foster the development of a learning community at the beginning of the school year. It identifies five ways to build a classroom culture in which children and adults see each other as resources for learning:

- Building a teaching team that supports your community of learners
- Offering more opportunities for small-group discussion
- Using documentation to promote collaboration
- Developing the capacity for peer feedback
- Involving students in what goes on the bulletin boards

Who Administrators, teacher leaders, and professional development providers can use this tool in staff meetings or as an introduction to MLV ideas for new teachers, student teachers, teaching assistants, paraprofessionals, classroom aides, parent volunteers, interested colleagues, and school visitors.

How This tool can be distributed to teachers or used in professional development sessions at the beginning of the school year to inform conversation about building learning groups in the classroom.

Variations and Extensions

- Pick one or two strategies to focus on and document.
- Brainstorm other ideas with colleagues.
- Create your own introduction to MLV ideas.
- Share the tool with parents to solicit their views.

Building a Teaching Team That Supports Your Community of Learners

You and your colleagues are a powerful model of collaboration for your students. Learners observe you discussing situations and solving problems. Ask teaching team members to participate in a group discussion or activity led by another adult. You can model collaborative comments and constructive feedback in class discussions. Such participation sends the message that everyone in the classroom is a member of the learning community.

Offering More Opportunities for Small-Group Discussion

It is easier for learners to discuss, debate, and share ideas in small groups. Small groups allow students with common interests and complementary skills to work together. Even during whole-group lessons, consider asking students to talk to their neighbors or get into small groups for focused conversations that can be shared back with the whole group.

Using Documentation to Promote Collaboration

Collaboration is not automatic. Although some students come to school ready to learn and work with peers, others arrive seeing classmates as the competition and the teacher as the sole source of knowledge. Documentation—notes, photographs, video, student work, partial transcripts of conversations—provides a powerful and engaging basis for group discussion about how well you are learning together. Looking at documentation lets students see how they are interacting and develop norms for collaboration. Documentation is also a powerful way to celebrate successful moments or advances in learning (highlighting collaborative learning in particular may lead to greater student investment). Consider posting documentation on a bulletin board as a way to share important aspects of your learning community with others.

Developing the Capacity for Peer Feedback

Students sharing strategies and insights with each other can often be more effective than adult instruction. Provide opportunities for peer feedback, ideally in small groups, when students can discuss work in progress such as block structures, scientific drawings, creative writing, and math problems. These discussions can develop the group's capacity to give helpful feedback and create a collective sense of high standards. Sharing one or two highlights from the feedback sessions with the whole group can also promote this kind of collaboration.

Involving Students in What Goes On the Bulletin Boards

Bulletin boards can be a powerful tool to make learning visible. Ask your students what part of their learning they most want to share with the school community. Add your own perspective to a board—through a title or a brief summary about what you are learning from your students' work. Consider including students' thoughts about their work—what was hard, surprising, or exciting. Provide a place for feedback from viewers, remembering that specific questions and invitations will elicit more useful feedback (ask students what they want to know).

2 LOOKING AT LEARNING IN GROUPS: CLASSROOM DISCUSSION GUIDELINES

Learners often have useful ideas about how they learn best. Based on an example of a learning group from a Reggio Emilia classroom, this tool offers one way to launch a discussion about individual and group learning.

Who These discussion questions can be adapted for students of any age.

How The beginning of the year is a good time to facilitate this type of discussion, either in a large or small group. You can record or summarize student responses and post or keep as a reference point (see "Variations and Extensions").

Preparation (Twenty to Twenty-Five Minutes)

- Choose a visual essay from the MLV book[1] that you think will be especially engaging for your students and prepare it for presentation (e.g., download PowerPoints from the MLV website, copy the essay, etc.). The City of Reggio (boys and girls) and Ring-Around-the-Rosy have worked well in the past and are available on the MLV website (pzweb.harvard.edu/mlv/documentation/indexd708.html). You can also use a learning portrait from this book.

- Practice reading the essay before presenting it to your students. Edit the narrative as appropriate for your age group.

- Think through the kind of conversation you hope to have with your students and questions you want to ask (suggestions following). What would you like to learn about your students' feelings and ideas about learning in groups? Jot down your hypotheses about how you think students will respond.

- How do you want to organize the presentation and discussion? Whole group? Small groups? Think about what forms of documentation will capture what you most want to learn. Choose at least two ways to document, such as a tape recorder and photographs or notes.

Presentation and Discussion (Thirty to Forty-Five Minutes)

- Before sharing the visual essay, ask students about their own experiences learning in groups:
  - What are some things you learn best by yourself?
  - What are some things you learn best in a group?

- Ask students to pay close attention to what they notice about how individuals in the visual essay work together, what they say, when they work alone, and so on.

- Present the visual essay.

- Facilitate a conversation. Ask students what they noticed, what struck or surprised them, and what questions came up. Choose from the following questions or come up with your own:
  - How did this group learn together?
  - Can you think of a group you have been a part of that worked well or helped you learn?
  - What are some of the signs that a group is working well together?
  - When you learn in a group, do you all learn the same thing?
  - How do you decide on things in a group?
  - Which do you like better—working or learning alone or in a group? Why?
  - What can be hard about learning in a group? Learning alone?
  - Pretend you're the teacher of this class and you want to put kids into groups to learn about _____. How would you do it? (What size groups? With friends or not? Gender? Mix of skills or interests? With or without adults?)
  - What things would you look for to determine whether people in a group were learning?
  - What advice would you give me if I wanted to document how you learn and think? Individually? In a group?
  - Do you have any questions for me?

If it is hard to get the conversation going, point to specific moments in the story and ask students what they notice.

Reflection

- As soon as you have a free moment, quickly review the documentation you gathered. Add any notes that will help you remember key moments or highlights that shed light on your questions about learning in groups.

- Get your documentation into a format you can share with one or more colleagues.

- Share your documentation and ask your colleagues for their interpretations. Choose one or more moments, observations, or interpretations to share back with your students.

Variations and Extensions

- Choose a different example of children (or adults) learning together to ground the discussion such as a transcript of a conversation from your classroom.

- Give students scripts from the visual essays, learning portraits, or a conversation transcript from your class and ask them to read different roles.

- Use the responses you get from students as a reference point for the rest of the year. Revisit them from time to time to see how you are doing as a group.

- Ask students to respond to some or all of the same questions at the end of the year and compare their responses.

- For younger children, use a video clip or photographs and provide simple prompts ("In this group, who would you want to be and why?")

If You Only Have Five Minutes . . .

- Ask learners to identify one constructive group-learning technique before beginning small-group work.

- Ask learners to choose one group-learning norm to attend to during their group work.

3 CONSIDERATIONS FOR FORMING SMALL GROUPS

Being intentional about the formation of small groups supports how and what individuals and the group learn. Although random assignments can be efficient and effective, it is often helpful to consider group composition and sometimes student input ahead of time. Of course, there is no simple formula. Depending on the nature and structure of the task, time frame, and learning goals for you or your students, different factors will come into play. The checklist given here identifies eight factors to keep in mind when forming groups.

How Group formation is driven by the demands of the task. The first step is to consider whether a task is group worthy. The next is to identify what kinds of skills and roles the task requires. Use the following checklist if you want to consider further the composition of a small group.

Group Formation Checklist

Size As group size expands, the opportunity for each learner to share and negotiate ideas decreases. Groups of three can add a level of complexity that groups of two may lack. Groups of three to four learners are more likely to generate complex interactions and potentially constructive conflict. Group size is determined in part by the capacity of the group to engage in productive work and conversation and to negotiate conflict. Ideally, groups should be small enough for each person to track the ideas and contributions of others.

Stability If contributing to collective knowledge is the goal of group work, then relatively stable small groups will work well (though they can occasionally be mixed up). If your focus is individual learning, group stability over time becomes less important. Jigsaw grouping[2] is a cooperative learning technique in which each student in a home group is responsible for specializing in one aspect of a learning unit. Students meet with members from other groups who are assigned the same aspect and, after mastering the material, they return to the home group to teach the others what they have learned. Jigsaw groups encourage students to take more responsibility for their learning and deepen their own understanding by teaching other students.

Gender and Cultural Background Gender and cultural background have a strong influence on how groups function and learn. Girls tend to prefer smaller groups than boys. Learners from diverse cultural backgrounds bring multiple perspectives that can enrich the conversation and expand students' awareness and understanding of different points of view.

115

Student Interests and Competencies Students' engagement in the topic influences their commitment to a task. Depending on the topic and the learning goals, consider bringing together learners with shared or complementary interests. Grouping students together with different (but not too different) levels of ability supports the learning of all group members. Depending on the task, you may want to include a range of competencies such as writing, drawing, math, facilitation, and leadership skills. Try putting together more verbal students with students who are more action oriented.

Friendship Sometimes friends work well in a group; sometimes they distract each other. Friendship can provide confidence in the face of novelty. Although friends may be more apt to disagree with each other than students who are not friends, the disagreements are also less likely to disturb the relationship and easier to resolve. Friends can also provide an especially attentive audience for work presented by their peers. Students who have been in multiple classes together are often skilled at drawing on each other's competencies (e.g., they know who is strong in math, art, facilitation, and so on).

Student Input Involving students in the formation of small groups can increase their commitment to the work and the group. There is a difference between asking, "With whom do you want to be?" and "With whom do you learn the best?" You can request student input as one consideration but still make the final decision yourself or with one or more students. Students may surprise you with the thoughtfulness of their suggestions. Feel free to share some or all of these considerations with students.

Variations and Extensions

- Along with students, develop a set of norms for the group (e.g., monitor your airtime; it is OK to disagree; equal participation). Ask pairs of students to serve as norm guardians from time to time to assess how the norms are working.
- Experiment with different kinds of groups as a way to learn more about students and forming more productive groupings. For example, create groups that are single sex or mixed sex, group together quiet children, put students of mixed ability into groups of four or fewer, or put students in a group with at least one other person with whom they work well.
- Facilitate a conversation with your students seeking their thoughts about different aspects of small-group formation such as friends, size, student input, and so on.
- Introduce or develop a rubric with students to assess individual and group work.
- Occasionally ask students to track their participation in small groups and analyze the results.

If You Only Have Five Minutes . . .

- Debrief after small-group work by asking learners to identify one thing that worked well and one thing they need to work on.

4 ENTRY-POINT CHARTS: ENGAGING ALL MEMBERS OF THE GROUP

Keeping all learners engaged can be a challenge over the course of a long unit. When learners lose interest in a topic, they can distract the group from the work at hand. Although teachers often think about ways to engage students before beginning a long unit or project, entry-point charts record these thoughts so they can be revisited, revised, or shared. The charts are designed to highlight the connections between the curriculum and student interests and strengths and identify the different contribution students can make. They also provide useful information when forming small groups.

Who Teachers, students, or families can fill out entry-point charts. Although you can complete an entry-point chart by yourself, conversation with colleagues will strengthen the content. If you team teach, you may want to fill out the chart separately and compare entries.

How Use a grid such as the charts shown on page 118 or an Excel spreadsheet to create your chart. Write your class list down one side. Create categories across the top for potential student connections or contributions to the study. Contributions can be content related (has visited Mexico; knows a lot about animals) or process related (helps keep small groups focused on tasks).

Variations and Extensions

- Ask students to add to or fill out the chart themselves.
- Make the chart public so students can use classmates as resources.
- Ask families to fill out the chart either for themselves or about their child.
- Entry-point charts are often filled out by teachers but you can also interview students before beginning a unit. Consider videotaping or otherwise documenting students' responses. Possible questions include the following:
  - What do you already know about _____?
  - Why is it important to study or learn about _____?
  - What would you like to know about _____?
  - How do you think we can find out about _____?
  - What do you think would be important for others to know about _____? How could we share it with them?
  - Do you have any concerns about studying _____?
  - How can I best support you in learning about _____?
  - What questions do you have for me?

Sample Charts

Ben Mardell used the grid shown in figure 9 to identify possible connections between his kindergarten students and their then-upcoming study of the Boston Marathon.

Figure 10 could be used to identify possible entry-points for a ninth grade study of *To Kill a Mockingbird* (a novel set in a small town in Alabama about racial prejudice, involving a trial). The last column represents responses to a student survey conducted at the beginning of the study (see "Variations and Extensions").

See figure 11 for a blank entry-point chart.

Student	Connection	Contribution
Addie	Interested in civil rights movement; might be interested in history of women runners	Strong group leader
Alex	Loves all things Italian; might be interested in Italian runners	Alex could help Mike overcome his shyness
Andrew	Loves hearing and telling stories	Ability to read and write
Christopher	Father ran the race; likes competition	Organizational skills, focus on task
Mike	Working with Alex might help him participate more	Encouraging and supportive group member

Figure 9. Ben Mardell's Entry-Point Chart

Student	Connection	Contribution	Student Survey
Paul	Family in Alabama	Good listener	Loves this book
Yusef	Mother is a lawyer	Graphic ability	No knowledge of book or story
Illana	Grandmother participated in civil rights movement	Knowledgeable about civil rights movement	Saw the movie
Sheniah	Loves to read	Strong writer	Would like to be in a leadership role

Figure 10. Entry-Point Chart for Ninth Grade Literature Class

Student	Connection	Contribution

Figure 11. Entry-Point Chart Template

5 STRUCTURES FOR GIVING AND RECEIVING FEEDBACK

This tool describes different structures for giving and receiving feedback, including feedback sessions, a critique center, and classroom routines. Giving and getting peer feedback gives learners an opportunity to do the following:

- See themselves as sources of knowledge who can guide and shape their own and their peers' learning
- Mark progress, reveal misconceptions, and revise thinking
- Develop their abilities to offer, accept, and negotiate different points of view
- Become more comfortable with assessment—often a sensitive topic

Who Cognitive conflict is often more constructive between students than between students and teachers, where the authority relationship is more pronounced. Feedback can come from another student, a small group, or a facilitated large-group discussion. Teachers can model the content and quality of feedback for learners.

How Feedback is most effective when it is grounded in an artifact (a draft paper, a painting, a diagram) that represents the learners' thinking, when it is solicited before the work is finished, and when the learner identifies specific questions to respond to.

Variations and Extensions

For the Primary Grades
- Introduce a critique center as a choice during center time with the following guidelines (from the Anser Charter School, Boise, Idaho):
  - Ask three friends for suggestions about your work.
  - *Three rules:* The suggestions have to be specific, kind, and helpful.
  - You don't have to follow the advice.
- At the beginning and end of center activities, ask learners to share work with their peers to get feedback and inspire ideas, using the following protocol. Prepare the presenter(s) ahead of time.
  - Looking (quiet looking at a child's work)
  - Noticing (I notice that . . . I see . . .)
  - Listening (presenting child speaks)

120

- Wondering (How did you . . . What did you . . . I wonder why . . .)
- Inspiring (friendly ideas to help improve or finish work)
- Post comments in the classroom made by students and adults as a reference for the group. For example:
  - I was inspired by . . .
  - Maybe . . .
  - I notice . . .
  - Another way you could do it is . . .
  - What if . . .
  - I wonder . . .
  - How could you . . .
  - I could . . .
- Begin a routine of ongoing informal opportunities for learners to give and receive feedback. Using everyday language, encourage learners to seek and offer feedback. "Are you sure the work is finished? Go ask _____ what she or he thinks about what you did." Toward the beginning of a task or activity, you can also ask learners to take two minutes to walk around the room to see how their classmates have begun.
- Invite other teachers, administrators, parents, or students into your classroom to offer feedback.

For Learners of Any Age
- See-think-wonder thinking routine:
  The see-think-wonder thinking routine, developed by Project Zero colleagues David Perkins, Ron Ritchhart, and Shari Tishman to explore works of art and other objects of interest, encourages participants to make careful observations and thoughtful interpretations by responding to three sentence stems: "I see . . ., I think . . ., I wonder . . ." As with the other protocols, the "I see . . ." comments are intended to be purely descriptive rather than interpretive or evaluative.
- What do you see?
- What do you think about that?
- What does it make you wonder?

The Ladder of Feedback

The ladder of feedback routine was developed by David Perkins and Daniel Wilson to provide constructive feedback about an idea, plan, behavior, or artifact. It includes four steps: clarify, value, share concerns, and suggest. The ladder can be conducted in a few minutes or used for more than an hour. (*Note:* Multiple versions exist online including a number of useful templates.)

Step 1: Clarify: Ask clarifying questions to be sure you understand the issue on the table. Avoid clarifying questions that are thinly disguised criticism.

Step 2: Value: Express what you like about the matter at hand in specific terms. Do not offer perfunctory "good, but . . ." and hurry onto the negatives.

Step 3: Share Concerns: Share your puzzles and concerns. Avoid absolutes: "What's wrong is . . ." Use qualified terms, "I wonder if . . ." "It seems to me . . ." Avoid criticizing personal character or ability and focus on ideas and products.

Step 4: Suggest: Make suggestions about how to improve things. This step is sometimes blended with step 3 (offer concerns along with suggestions for addressing them).

If You Only Have Five Minutes . . .

- Invite students to turn to a peer and raise one question about their own work with which they are struggling.

Feedback Sessions for Middle and High School Students

Hold feedback, critique, or work-share sessions once or twice a week to look at unfinished work. Small groups of three to four students usually work better than a large group. Begin by modeling the feedback process with the whole group. Role-play with your students what constructive and nonconstructive feedback look like. Post key vocabulary or sentence starters in your room. Sessions can be structured in the following ways:

- Ask students to explain where the work is coming from. If the work is in response to a particular assignment, students might name what learning goals the work is supposed to demonstrate or what they think the teacher is looking for. If the work is purely student generated (students have generated all the goals for the work), students can identify what they were hoping to achieve. In either case, students should begin by commenting on their own work and specifying what in particular they would like feedback on. Adults can participate in the conversation and model helpful feedback.
- Ask the group the following questions:
  - Look carefully at the work with a focus on describing, not judging or interpreting. (What do you see in this drawing? What do you notice about this essay?) If students do make a judgment or interpretation, ask what in the work makes them say that.
  - What questions do you have for the creator of the work? (Why did the artist put blue on the face? How is the writer supporting his or her claim?)
  - What suggestions do you have for what to do next? (What might help the drawing be more realistic? What might make the essay stronger? Is there something in someone else's work that you wish _____ had included, too?)
- For analytical or problem-solving work, learners can use the following sentence starters:
  - This work seems finished to me because _____.
  - One thing I think our teacher will think is really good is _____.
  - One thing I think is really good is _____.

122

- One thing I think you should look over again or work on a little more is _____ because _____. Or, here's a place where I think you could improve this a little by _____.
- One thing about your work that is really interesting or helpful to me is _____.

Document some or all of the session via video, audio, or notes and photographs. Share selected parts of the documentation at the next session to reflect on what is working well and what can be improved.

If You Only Have Five Minutes . . .

- Invite students to turn to a peer and raise one question about their own work with which they are struggling.

Chapter 12
Supporting Learning in Groups in the Staffroom

This chapter includes a hands-on activity for adults to explore learning groups and documentation, a tool for forming adult study groups, and protocols for discussing and reflecting on student learning. Protocols are structures that guide conversation. The protocols in tools 7 through 10 encourage close observation and analysis of documentation with a focus on deepening understanding of student learning. Documentation grounds the conversation in a shared reference point that people can draw on to support or challenge an interpretation. Often the documenters whose work is being discussed remain quiet while the rest of the group shares its thoughts so the documenters can truly listen to and learn from the multiple perspectives of others.

Tool 6. "Throwing Your Money Away": Exploring Group Learning and Documentation
This is an interactive activity in which adult learners take on the roles of group learners and documenters in order to explore the relationship between individual and group learning and how documentation can support learning.

Tool 7. Designing and Facilitating Adult Study Groups
In this tool, we identify considerations for designing and facilitating adult study groups and suggest discussion questions and a sample meeting agenda.

Tool 8. Looking at Documentation: The Collaborative Assessment Conference
This protocol is designed for teachers who want to review student work or documentation in a structured conversation that progresses from observation and description to interpretation and speculation.

Tool 9. Creating Documentation for Public Viewing: Protocol 1
This protocol is for teachers who are at the beginning of creating documentation to be shared publicly and who want feedback from colleagues.

Tool 10. Creating Documentation for Public Viewing: Protocol 2
This protocol follows the previous protocol and is designed for teachers who are further along in the documentation creation process.

6 "THROWING YOUR MONEY AWAY": EXPLORING GROUP LEARNING AND DOCUMENTATION

This tool is designed to engage people quickly in solving a problem and building understanding (in this case about aerodynamics) in order to ground conversation about individual and group learning. The activity offers a low-stakes way for adult learners to gain direct experience with MLV ideas and practices. Learners consider what and how people learn in groups and the role of documentation in supporting group learning by taking on the roles of group learners and documenters. Participants are asked to reflect on documentation as a process of observing, recording, interpreting, and sharing information with learners and as a way to shape future learning experiences.

Who This activity is designed for administrators, teacher leaders, professional development facilitators, and others who work with adult learners. It can also be used with parents, guardians, and older students to ground a discussion about the role of documentation in learning groups.

How The activity takes about thirty-five to forty-five minutes and requires the following materials (exact amounts depend on the size of the group): 8.5" × 11" paper, scissors, Scotch tape, paper clips, pennies, wooden coffee stirrers, pencils, and markers. Small groups of four to five usually work well. Make sure that there are at least two documenters and two learners per small group.

125

Step 1: The Activity (Fifteen to Twenty Minutes)

Divide participants into small groups of four to five. Ask participants to introduce themselves to each other.

Instructions for learners: You will have twelve to fifteen minutes to come up with two different designs for paper airplanes that can fly at least ten feet carrying at least five pennies.

Instructions for documenters: Please observe with the following question in mind: What do you notice about the individuals' and group's process of building knowledge and what can you point to that makes you say that? Watch for interesting or important moments or shifts in the ways ideas are being developed. Afterward, describe and interpret how those moments advanced the knowledge building of the group. Document your observations individually. You can document in any way you wish—jot down bits of conversation, take pictures with your cell phone, write short descriptive notes, or draw pictures or diagrams—but you must document in some way!

Step 2: Debriefing in Small Groups (Ten to Twelve Minutes)

Documenters: Share with the learners selected observations and documentation about the individuals' and group's process of building knowledge. Try to identify interesting or important moments or shifts in the ways ideas were being developed and offer an interpretation of how they advanced the learning process.

Learners: Share your responses to the documenters' observations and interpretations as well as your own reflections regarding interesting or important moments or shifts in the learning process and what you learned about aerodynamics.

As a small group: Choose one thing you learned about the principles of aerodynamics and one thing you learned about individual and group learning or the process of documentation to share with the whole group. Feel free to walk around and look at the designs of other groups.

Step 3: Whole-Group Discussion (Ten Minutes)

Small groups each report one thing they learned about aerodynamics and one thing they learned about individual and group learning or the process of documentation. As time allows, you can also ask small groups to discuss the following questions:

- What did you notice or learn because of the documentation being shared?
- What might you do with—or how might you use—this information in another experience with these learners or in your own classroom?

7 DESIGNING AND FACILITATING ADULT STUDY GROUPS

Even if you are committed to creating an adult study group to look at documentation of student learning, it can be hard to know where to start. This tool identifies key features to consider when launching adult study groups. It also includes a sample agenda and discussion protocol for looking at documentation of student learning.

Who This tool is most useful for administrators, professional development providers, or teacher leaders who facilitate adult study groups such as classroom teams, grade-level colleagues, members of an academic department, or colleagues from different schools.

How Consider the following elements when forming adult study groups.

Group Size and Composition
Determine size of the group (ideally four to eight participants) and criteria for group membership depending on your goal (e.g., interest in the topic, similarity or diversity of grade level or subject matter, or variety of perspectives).

Length and Frequency of Meetings
Decide on length and frequency of meetings—ideally at least forty-five to sixty minutes and once or twice a month.

Rotation Schedule
Create a rotation schedule in which one to two individuals or teams share documentation at each meeting.

Documentation Guidelines
Propose guidelines for selecting and sharing documentation:

- Ask participants to identify a focus question about teaching and learning to guide their inquiry (see tool 12 in chapter 13). Although posing a question about teaching and learning often helps to focus the collection and selection of documentation, sometimes teachers prefer to document in a more open-ended fashion to see what emerges (see tool 13 in chapter 13).
- Put your documentation into an easily shareable format such as PowerPoint or video that can be shown on a laptop or projected, or make copies of text and images for the entire group to look at. Video clips should be fewer than five minutes and, ideally, viewed twice. Written documents should be able to be read in three to five minutes.
- Keep context brief (two to three minutes).
- Choose a protocol or thinking routine for discussing the documentation.

Group Norms

With the group, identify group norms such as the following:
- Start and end on time
- Ensure equal participation (go-arounds can be useful here)
- Rotate roles such as note taking, time keeping, facilitating, and monitoring norms

Notes

Think about how to capture what the group is learning for its own use or for sharing with others.

Sample Meeting Agenda (Thirty to Thirty-Five Minutes)

- Review meeting goals, group norms, agenda, and notes or highlights from the last meeting. (two minutes)
- Participants give brief classroom updates since last meeting. (three to five minutes)
- Presenter provides brief context. (three minutes)
- Group asks presenter clarifying questions. (two minutes)
- Group looks at documentation in silence. (three to five minutes)
- Group responds to following questions while presenter is silent. (ten to twelve minutes)
  - What do you see or hear in the documentation? Point to what makes you say that.
  - What questions does the documentation raise? (Presenter does not answer questions.)
  - What are the implications for teaching and learning and next steps for the presenter?
- Presenter shares his or her take-aways. (two minutes)
- Group members jot down at least one idea to use in their own classrooms and share ideas with the group. (four minutes)
- Debrief protocol and thank presenter. (one minute)

Variations and Extensions

- Presenters may prefer to name one or two questions when giving a brief context for more specific group feedback.
- Experiment with different amounts of time for looking at the work and the protocol as a whole. What do you notice when you spend more or less time with the protocol?
- The following is another possible set of discussion questions for when the group responds. Identify two or three focus questions in the following that one or more of the group is most interested in exploring.

What Are Students Learning and Understanding?

- What are the key concepts or skills the students are working on?
- What evidence do you see of student learning?

How Is the Group Learning?

- How do the interactions or conversations among students help them learn or make learning more difficult? (Consider size and composition of the group, the language and strategies used, the roles students take, and what they choose to share with each other.)
- When does one person's thinking seem to affect the thinking of another or the whole group?
- What does the documentation suggest about creating better conditions (physical space, time, materials, nature of the task, etc.) for learning in groups?

Where Do You Go Next?

- What might you try next to deepen or extend students' thinking or learning?
- What might be the value of sharing some or all of this documentation and perhaps your own reflections with the students? What might you select and how might you frame it?
- What is still puzzling or interesting to you after viewing the documentation?

Tools 8 through 10 provide other discussion protocols from which to choose. You can also visit www.makinglearningvisibleresources.org or www.schoolreforminitiative.org for additional options.

If You Only Have Five Minutes . . .

- Start a routine of sharing a short video clip or other example of student documentation at the beginning of staff meetings.
- Start staff meetings with five minutes in which anyone can ask for help with a dilemma and get quick feedback or brainstorming.
- Invite a colleague into your classroom when something unusual is going on.
- Display documentation in the teachers' room over the course of a week with a note asking colleagues to share what they see, think, or wonder on sticky notes.

 ## 8 LOOKING AT DOCUMENTATION: THE COLLABORATIVE ASSESSMENT CONFERENCE

The Collaborative Assessment Conference (CAC) protocol was developed in 1988 by Steve Seidel and colleagues at Project Zero. The CAC helps teachers examine and discuss student work or documentation in a structured conversation that progresses from observation and description to speculation and interpretation. It is an excellent protocol for focusing tightly on one piece of documentation and practicing skills of observation and description.

Who This protocol can be used by any group of educators or other adults who want to understand student work more deeply.

How Choose a facilitator to guide the group through the steps of the protocol and keep track of time. Ask the facilitator to begin by explaining the rationale for the protocol and reviewing the steps with the group. Facilitators should also ask participants to refrain from making judgments or assumptions about the documentation. If participants do make assumptions or evaluative comments, the facilitator should ask, "What in this work leads you to say that?" Post the protocol or make copies for the group. Most protocols end with thanking the presenter and debriefing the protocol, even if just with a thumbs up or thumbs down. If, after trying a protocol several times, you find that the structure inhibits rather than enhances conversation, put the protocol aside. The CAC protocol takes about an hour.

Getting Started

The conference begins with everyone present silently looking at the documentation that the presenting teachers have brought.

Describing the Work

The group is asked to describe any noteworthy aspects of the documentation, withholding judgments of quality and comments about taste ("I like . . ." or "I don't like . . .").

Raising Questions

Once everyone has had a chance to describe the work, the group is asked to state any questions that arose during the first phase of the conference. Remind the group they may not get answers to all of their questions. What's important is noticing what questions and issues the documentation raises.

Speculating about What the Students Are Working On

At this point, the group is asked to make some guesses—and explain the thinking behind the guesses—about what the students were working on in this documentation.

Hearing from the Presenting Teachers

The presenting teachers now add their perspectives on the previous phases of the conference: description, questions raised, and speculation about what students were working on. They may or may not choose to respond to all of the questions raised by the group.

Discussing Implications for Teaching and Learning

Everyone is invited to share thoughts provoked by this discussion about teaching and learning and ways to support individual and group learning.

Reflecting on the Protocol

Leave time at the end of the conference to reflect more generally on the process—what was helpful in the protocol and what was frustrating?

Thanks!

End the session with acknowledgment and thanks to the presenting teachers and the facilitator.

Variations and Extensions

Visit www.schoolreforminitiative.org or www.pzweb.harvard.edu/vt for other examples of protocols and thinking routines. Thinking routines are simple, easy-to-use structures such as a short sequence of steps or questions designed to foster thinking skills and dispositions and to deepen learning. If you are short on time, see-think-wonder and the ladder of feedback are good routines to use with students or colleagues (see tool 5 in chapter 11).

9 CREATING DOCUMENTATION FOR PUBLIC VIEWING: PROTOCOL 1

This tool is a short protocol for use early in the documentation process. It is helpful for looking at student work or documentation in progress that will be shared with learners or others during or after a learning experience. Allow approximately twenty-five minutes for each piece of documentation.

Who This protocol is useful for teachers who are at the beginning of the process of creating documentation to be shared with learners or others.

How Choose a facilitator to guide the group through the protocol and keep track of time. Ask the facilitator to begin by explaining the rationale for the protocol and reviewing the steps with the group. Post the protocol or make copies for the group. End by thanking the presenter and debriefing the protocol, even if just with a thumbs up or thumbs down.

- Documenter(s) verbally shares contextual information for the documentation. (two minutes)
- Group looks at the documentation in silence. (three to five minutes)
- Group asks clarifying questions. (two minutes)
- Group provides feedback on the documentation, keeping the following questions in mind, and the documenter(s) remains silent and takes notes. (ten minutes)
    - Who are the members of the learning group in this documentation?
    - What do they seem to be learning in this experience?
    - How are they learning with and from each other?
    - What in this documentation grabs your attention or feels especially compelling?
    - How does the documentation communicate this?
- Documenter(s) share a last thought or take-away. (two minutes)
- Group thanks documenter(s) for bringing the work. (one minute)
- Group reflects on the usefulness of the protocol. (two minutes)

Variations and Extensions

- Adjust the timing of the protocol depending on the time you have available and the number of people sharing work.
- Adjust the questions in the protocol to focus on your own questions and areas of interest.
- If finding time to meet with colleagues proves difficult, experiment with sharing documentation online via a site like VoiceThread.com or posting documentation in the teachers' lounge or other common areas and asking your colleagues to provide feedback on sticky notes.

10 CREATING DOCUMENTATION FOR PUBLIC VIEWING: PROTOCOL 2

This tool is another relatively quick protocol for teachers who are creating documentation to be shared publicly, such as on bulletin boards, exhibit panels, or video.

Who This protocol is useful for teachers or others who are creating documentation for public viewing and who are at least midway through the process.

How Choose a facilitator to guide the group through the protocol and keep track of time. Ask the facilitator to begin by explaining the rationale for the protocol and reviewing the steps with the group. Post the protocol or make copies for the group. End the protocol by thanking the presenter and debriefing the protocol, even if just with a thumbs up or thumbs down. This protocol runs about twenty-five to thirty minutes.

- Documenter(s) says which two of the three areas for feedback are of greatest interest (focus on learning, interpretation and support for interpretation, or the viewer's experience). (one minute)
- Documenter(s) shows documentation to the group without providing a verbal introduction of any kind. The group looks at the documentation without talking. (five to seven minutes)
- Group offers feedback on the two areas selected by the documenter(s) and the documenter(s) remains silent. (ten minutes)
    - *Focus on learning:* In what ways does the documentation focus on learning, not just something "we did"? How does it make the learning process as well as the product visible? How might it promote conversation or deepen understanding about some aspect of learning?
    - *Interpretation and support for interpretation:* What interpretation by teachers or students does the documentation include? What evidence for this or other interpretations does the documentation provide?
    - *The viewer's experience:* Are the viewers learning what they need to know in order to follow the account of learning represented in the documentation? Do the visual components add to or detract from the viewers' experience?

- Documenter(s) shares a last thought and responds to the question, "Am I clear about what to work on? If so, what is it? If not, what will I do to get clear?" (three to five minutes)
- Group thanks documenter(s) for bringing the work. (one minute)
- Group reflects on usefulness of the protocol. (two minutes)

Variations and Extensions

- Adjust the timing to the amount you have available and the number of people sharing the work. See-think-wonder is a good protocol if you are short on time (see tool 5 in chapter 11).
- Adjust the questions in the protocol to focus on your own questions and areas of interest.
- If finding time to meet with colleagues proves difficult, experiment with sharing documentation online via a site like VoiceThread.com.

Chapter 13
Documenting Individual and Group Learning

This chapter includes resources for understanding, creating, and sharing documentation with students and colleagues. Some tools are designed to help teachers identify a purpose for their documentation; others provide guidelines for gathering or sharing documentation via video, computer, or photographs.

Tool 11. Documentation: When Does It Make Learning Visible?
The questions in this tool guide the creation, collection, and examination of documentation that attempts to make learning visible for one's own reflection, for sharing back with learners, and for sharing more widely.

Tool 12. Beginning to Document through Intentional Inquiry
Here, we describe a protocol for choosing a guiding question to focus observations while documenting.

Tool 13. Beginning to Document by Stepping Back
This tool suggests another way to begin documenting with a more open stance.

Tool 14. Considerations for Selecting a Documentation Tool
This resource identifies considerations for choosing from a range of documentation tools such as notes, photos, video, and audio recorder.

Tool 15. Guidelines for Shooting Video or Photographs
These guidelines and technical considerations are helpful for capturing better video and photographs.

Tool 16. Making Learners' Words Visible: Speech Bubbles
In this tool, we suggest a way to make learners' words and thinking visible through photographs and speech bubbles. Speech bubbles provide a visible reference and reminder to learners (and others) of key ideas or moments in their learning.

11 DOCUMENTATION: WHEN DOES IT MAKE LEARNING VISIBLE?

Not all documentation makes learning visible. The criteria for documentation that makes learning visible depend on the context. Documentation serves different purposes during different stages of learning. What seems to remain constant is that quality documentation focuses on some aspect of learning—not just "what we did"—and prompts questions and promotes conversation among children and adults that deepen and extend learning.

How The following questions guide the collection, examination, and creation of documentation that makes learning visible in three contexts: documenting for your own reflection, for sharing back with learners, and for sharing more widely. The questions may change depending on your purpose or context.

For Collecting Documentation to Aid Your Own Reflection
- Am I documenting my own words and actions as well as the students'?
- Does the documentation help me reexamine things I did not initially notice or understand?
- Does it help me identify key moments of learning or aspects of the learning context?
- Does it suggest next steps for teaching or learning?
- Does it raise questions I can discuss with my colleagues or students?
- What other documentation might I collect to extend this inquiry? Would my documentation be strengthened by using more than one medium?

For Sharing Documentation with Students or Colleagues
- Does the documentation focus on learning, not just something we did?
- Does it promote conversation or deepen understanding about some aspect of teaching and learning?
- Does it help me address a particular question I have about learning?
- When is an appropriate time to share the documentation with my students and what might we learn?

For Documentation That Is to Be Shared More Widely

- Does the documentation provide enough context for the viewer to understand the piece?
- Does it focus on learning, not just on what was done?
- Does it focus on the process as well as the product(s) of learning?
- Does it clearly communicate the aspects of learning I consider most important?
- Does it include an interpretation by teachers and/or students?
- Does it include more than one medium?
- Does the documentation add to our collective body of knowledge and promote conversation about learning?
- Is it presented in a way that draws the viewer in?
- Does it have an engaging title?

12 BEGINNING TO DOCUMENT THROUGH INTENTIONAL INQUIRY

There are many ways to get started with documentation. Some teachers begin by identifying a question about learning they want to explore. Others wait until a classroom need arises that can be addressed by documentation. Still others decide to cast a wide net and observe or videotape a session without a particular purpose in mind, just to see what of interest emerges. Regardless of how you start, it is important to be clear in your own mind about why you are documenting and what you want to learn from it. Tools 12 and 13 describe two different ways to start documenting—one more intentional and one more exploratory. (Tool 1 in chapter 11 and tool 8 in chapter 12 suggest additional ways to become familiar with documentation.)

Who The choosing-a-question protocol[1] is useful for teachers formulating a question about individual and group learning to guide their documentation.

How The protocol can be used by a small or large group. Allow at least thirty to forty minutes; however, in larger groups the discussion may take longer.

- Decide if you want to identify a shared question. Questions can be developed individually, with partners, or as a whole group. (three minutes)
- Consider the following criteria for each candidate question (ten to fifteen minutes). Is your question
  - Connected to supporting individual and group learning?
  - Connected to your own educational values and interests?
  - Related to your school's mission or educational values?
  - Likely to be of interest and value to other educators?
  - Related to a topic that students could help you investigate?
  - A manageable size (e.g., grounded in something you already do in the classroom)?
  - Aesthetically pleasing to you and others (e.g., succinct, inspiring)?
- Write your question on chart paper. The group shares thoughts about the question in relation to these criteria (except the connection to your educational values and interests) and you remain silent. (fifteen to twenty minutes)
- Presenter shares main take-aways. (one to two minutes)
- Facilitator thanks the presenter(s).
- Repeat this process for each question in your group.
- Debrief the protocol. (two minutes)

13 BEGINNING TO DOCUMENT BY STEPPING BACK

The following exercise suggests beginning to document by stepping back to observe and listen to learners with a sense of curiosity and wonder, remaining open to the unexpected.

How In your classroom, select a moment to observe or listen to and record one or more student's thinking or learning process. Think ahead to what form your documentation will take—paper and pencil, camera, audio recorder. Choose a format with which you are comfortable. Consider filling out the "Beginning to Document Planning Worksheet" at the end of this tool.

Choose a Time When . . .

- Learners are exploring a new material or grappling with a new idea.
- Learners say or do something that puzzles or surprises you.
- Learners are discussing a text, planning a project, or reacting to a story you've read. What comments do they make? What questions do they ask? Feel free to probe the learners' thinking (as long as you also document your own words or actions).

Whether you choose one of these contexts or another one, arrange to observe and record what learners do and say along with your own thoughts about what learners might be thinking or learning.

What Next?
Write about the experience as soon as you can. If possible, review the documentation you collected (notes, photographs, video, audio, your own reflections) with colleagues. What do you make of what the learners said or did? What thinking or learning can you detect? What questions come up? What might you try next?

Variations and Extensions

- When you document, look for learners making connections, collaborative learning, voices that are seldom heard, ideas that advance thinking, key questions, misconceptions, assumptions, disagreements, apparent contradictions, diverse responses, or anything that could benefit from revisiting.
- Document when things are either going exceptionally well or unusually poorly.
- Consider sharing part of the documentation with the learners.

- With elementary or older students, choose a time when you can step back and let the students lead the class while you observe and document.
- Invite students to document selected learning moments to share back with the class.

If You Only Have Five Minutes . . .

- Share back a quote from a learner during the next class.
- Take a photograph of something that piques your interest and post it on a wall.
- Show a short video clip, perhaps from the previous day's activities, to remind learners of an important learning moment.

Beginning to Document Planning Worksheet

What will you observe?

Whom will you observe?

Where will you observe?

When will you observe?

What documentation tools will you use (paper and pencil, camera, audio recorder, etc.)?

What do you think you might see or hear?

Which colleagues will you ask to look at the documentation with you? When and where?

14 CONSIDERATIONS FOR SELECTING A DOCUMENTATION TOOL

Teachers often need to make decisions about which documentation tools to use based on convenience or availability. But different types of learning events and activities call for different types of documentation tools, which, in turn, support different forms of communication. The following guidelines help teachers become familiar with the advantages and limitations of different documentation tools.

Who Although these considerations are intended primarily for teachers and other adults (parents, grandparents, community volunteers), students—even young children, with training—can also gather documentation. Asking students to document can show teachers the student's perspective about what's worth paying attention to, reveal hidden group dynamics, and foster a greater sense of student ownership of the documentation and perhaps learning. Involving students is especially useful for engaging students who otherwise struggle in group activities.

How Although taking notes is perhaps the most common form of documentation, other useful media include still and video cameras, digital audio recorders, cell phones, and laptops. Here, we identify key considerations for collecting documentation using video, photography, and other tools in order to support student learning and make it visible. The documentation process generally follows six steps:

- Identifying a focus
- Selecting a documentation tool
- Collecting the documentation
- Shaping the documentation to share with colleagues
- Identifying a useful conversation structure
- Using documentation to inform next steps or share back with learners

This tool focuses on the second step of selecting a tool for documentation. Tool 15 offers technical advice for shooting video and photographs. (See tools 7 through 10 in chapter 12 for information related to the other steps.)

Considerations for Selecting a Documentation Tool

Still Photographs Along with communicating information (such as who was there, what were they doing, etc.), photographs can convey deeper meanings. Choose a still camera when you want to capture particular moments or qualities of an experience that can be easily revisited (and recounted) with students or others. For those who were present, an image is often enough to spark memories and personal accounts. For those who were not there, images can capture the emotional and aesthetic qualities of an experience and draw them in.

One strength of photographs is that they can focus attention on a single or series of moments and deepen observation and analysis. They slow us down and encourage reflection. However, photographs can also limit our observation and analysis to the moment captured—a fragment of what video might record.

If the audible aspects of an experience or activity are important, video is often preferable. You can also audio record or take notes to accompany your images.

Video Video affords the possibility of capturing the visual and audio aspects of an experience in a less fragmented way than still images. Video is particularly useful for capturing action, facial expressions, body language, gestures, dialogue, tone, and group dynamics. Teachers of infants and toddlers are often drawn to video because very young children express themselves primarily through their actions. Although video is a good choice for documenting in many circumstances, there are also downsides.

Logistically it is hard for many teachers to find the time to take video (versus taking an occasional still photo), watch it (a good reason to be selective about what you shoot), and process it (download it to your computer and perhaps edit it into shareable form). Videotaping while talking or facilitating at the same time is an acquired skill but well worth practicing because it enables a more seamless approach to documentation. Other options include using a laptop, setting up a video camera on a tripod, or asking a colleague or student to videotape. Although video is not as easy to share with others as still images, it provides a less filtered view of events and more opportunity for getting a perspective different from your own.

Cameras that use tapes can be expensive (unless you reuse the tapes), but tapes are easier to store than files. Digital cameras that record to an internal memory or memory card require you to download your files between shoots so you will have available memory for next time. File sizes can be large so computer storage space becomes an issue. On the plus side, there are many tools available now for shooting video that make it easy to shoot, download, and share. Experiment with using Photo Booth on a Macintosh laptop, a point-and-shoot camera that shoots still images as well as good video, or your cell phone.

Typed and Handwritten Notes The simplest and lowest-tech way to document is taking typed or handwritten notes. Notes capture student thinking via quotes, excerpts from conversations, observations, or quick sketches of work in progress and make them immediately available for reflection or sharing with colleagues or learners. Many teachers type notes on their laptops during whole- or small-group conversations. If you are a fast typist, you can capture much of what is said almost verbatim. If you prefer handwriting, you can focus on capturing key words and going back to your notes at your earliest opportunity to fill in the blanks.

Note-taking is also an effective way to capture your thinking—which is not possible when videotaping unless you speak directly to the camera. Notes complement still images well; images can prompt thoughts to jot down in a notebook or directly on printed photographs. You can also annotate the images digitally using an application such as thinglink.com. Annotating photographs is also a good student reflection or documentation activity.

Note-taking can take place privately or publicly. Black- or whiteboards, chart paper, or laminated speech bubbles (see variations in tool 16) are all useful resources for public note-taking. Students or colleagues can help out as well. Another strategy is to keep notebooks, sticky notes, or other writing material in strategic places for capturing memorable moments and quotes. Some teachers wear an apron with pockets for a notebook, pencils, and camera.

Audio Recorder A digital audio recorder is also useful for capturing conversations and the auditory aspects of events and activities. Audio recorders are easier to operate and have a lower profile than a video (or even still) camera. People often forget that an audio recorder is there. Teachers can easily turn on a recorder at the beginning of a conversation or activity and let it run until the end.

Like video, audio recorders work in real time so you can end up with half an hour or more of material to listen to later. If you are present, one trick to save time is to jot down the time when you begin recording and the times of any moments that stand out to you to which you would like to return.

Recorded audio is also a bit awkward to share. You can play it directly (which requires knowing the exact location of the section you want to listen to or skipping around in the recording) or transcribe portions of the recording (which is easier for sharing, but is also time consuming and loses important qualities such as tone of voice).

If You Only Have Five Minutes . . .

- Jot down a provocative or insightful comment made by a student and share it with the class.
- Take a photograph of an especially powerful learning moment to revisit with students.
- Take a photograph of a student's moment of success and put it on the wall.
- Share a few moments of video of a previous lesson before you begin the current lesson.

15 GUIDELINES FOR SHOOTING VIDEO AND PHOTOGRAPHS

....

This tool identifies guidelines and additional resources for shooting video and photographs and related technical considerations.

Who These guidelines are intended primarily for teachers or other adults and students interested in using video and still cameras to document student learning. Keep in mind that most cell phones, iPads, and laptops can be used to shoot video and still images, too. Make sure you check the school's policy regarding permissions before shooting.

How Use the following guidelines for shooting more intentional and effective video and photographs.

Getting Organized

If your camera uses tapes, label each new tape before you use it (date, subject, etc.). When the tape is full, shift the switch on the tape from record mode (closed) to save mode (open) to avoid accidentally recording over a tape. If your camera records to a flash card or internal drive, name each clip or file as soon as you download it to your computer. Make sure your battery is charged and that you have enough tape or memory on your camera's hard drive or flash card.

Use a Tripod to Get a Steady Shot

A tripod is extremely useful. If you're shooting a subject that is somewhat stationary (such as a group working around a table, a conversation you are facilitating and can't find someone else to shoot, an interview, etc.), a tripod will help you to maintain a steady shot. Tripods can also allow you to record something without physically being there. If you don't have a tripod, find another way to steady your camera, such as putting it on a table or stack of books. Gorilla pods are an inexpensive and versatile form of tripod (go to www.joby.com).

Preparing to Shoot

Always test your audio before you shoot by either wearing headphones or shooting for several seconds and playing it back. Move the camera in close to the action to pick up adequate audio. Don't talk when you're shooting unless you want to include your voice in your video.

Pay Attention to the Light

Avoid areas of high contrast such as dark and light settings or bright sunlight and shadows. Always shoot with the sun or windows to your back. Hold your hand over the top of the camera lens if the sun is directly overhead. If you can't avoid shooting toward the light, use the camera's back-light setting if it has one.

Compose Your Shots

Frame your shot so your subject is always highlighted. Who or what is most important at the moment? Try to shoot against a plain background so other objects will not compete for attention.

Hold Your Shots

Hold your shot for five seconds or more before moving the camera or zooming in or out. Excessive panning and zooming is hard to watch. Practice zooming in and out slowly and smoothly. Keep in mind that this is harder to do on small cameras with tiny controls.

Change Angles and Perspectives

Avoid shooting everything at eye level or from the same distance. Change the point of view or angle frequently. This will make it easier to cut between shots when editing. Look for interesting perspectives such as holding your camera low and shooting up toward your subject. (Shooting subjects from above diminishes them and puts the videographer in a position of power.) The small size of digital video cameras makes these shots easy to take. Close-up shots help viewers feel connected to the subject and to see key details. This is especially important when showing video in a small format, such as on the web. Wide-angle shots will not display much detail in a small window.

Most people take pictures quickly, without much deliberation. Yet with a little thought, photographs can become much more evocative. Use the following guidelines for shooting more intentional and effective photographs.

Composing Your Picture

Use size, proximity, lines, and color to lead the eye to the main subject of your photograph. Diagonal lines and lighter and warmer colors attract the eye more than darker and cooler colors. Facial expressions and gestures can convey emotion and thinking. For a more dynamic composition, avoid putting your main subject in the center of the photograph. Use the rule of thirds—imagine a tic-tac-toe grid over your image and place your subject on one of the four points where the lines intersect.

Frame your shots intentionally so they include only what you think should be there. Shoot against a plain background and minimize clutter. Remove objects that seem to be coming out of your subject's head. Including things in the foreground can create a frame around the edges, adding visual interest and context for the photo. Consider horizontal and vertical possibilities.

Proximity to Your Subject

Move in closer to your subject to see more detail or convey intimacy. Move farther away to show context, emphasize a group interaction, or highlight aspects of the surrounding environment. Experiment with how the image changes when you are at, above, or below eye level. A good rule of thumb is to photograph children and other human subjects at eye-level or lower.

Decisions about Lighting

Natural light adds mood and depth to photographs whereas electronic flash flattens them. Turn off your flash whenever possible. In low-light situations, try turning the flash off and holding the camera steady to capture ambient light, use a tripod, or put your camera on a solid surface. You can also adjust your ISO (the light sensitivity) to eight hundred or higher. Know your flash range (usually no more than ten feet or about four steps). You can get close-up shots with a flash by zooming in rather than moving in too close for your flash. Outdoors, try to shoot early or late in the day or in the shade at midday. Use a flash for light fill if your subject is in shadow unless that is the effect you want.

Variations and Extensions

- Before starting to document, try to anticipate the types of activities you will encounter.

- When filming groups of children, start with wide-angle shots to establish the context. Perhaps hold the camera above your head to get an aerial view on the scene. Then move in closer to get shots from over children's shoulders, close-ups of their hands at work, low-angle shots looking up at them, and close-up facial shots. For example, if children are painting at an easel, capture the expressions on their faces, the way they hold their hands, the colors they are drawn to, and their interactions with each other and their paintings.

- Edit some of your video into a short three- to five-minute clip to share back with students, parents, colleagues, and others.

- If you're having a difficult time, try asking a tech-savvy student.

There are many easy video editing programs available. All Macs come with iMovie, and Movie Maker is the free editing software for PCs. Search in Google or YouTube for editing tutorials specific to your computer and the version of software you have. Here are a few links that we have found useful:

iMovie: www.apple.com/support/imovie, http://desktopvideo.about.com/od/imovievideotutorials/iMovie_Video_Tutorials_Learn_How_to_Use_iMovie_From_Video_Tutorials.htm

Movie Maker: http://windows.microsoft.com/en-US/windows-vista/Getting-started-with-Windows-Movie-Maker, www.atomiclearning.com/moviemaker2

Uploading video to the web: http://desktopvideo.about.com/od/videoonyourwebsite/bb/b4upload.htm

General: www.lynda.com (some free tutorials, others available only to paid subscribers)

Equipment reviews: www.dpreview.com, www.digitalcamerainfo.com, www.kenrockwell.com

16 MAKING LEARNERS' WORDS VISIBLE: SPEECH BUBBLES

Speech bubbles are just what they sound like. They usually take the form of a photograph or image of a child's head with a bubble containing the child's words. Speech bubbles support reflection and deepen learning by the following:

- Providing a visible reference and reminder to learners of key ideas or moments in their learning
- Making individual thinking visible and accessible to the group (revealing multiple perspectives)
- Enabling the group to revisit key moments of group learning
- Celebrating and strengthening a group's identity as a learning group

Who The learners themselves are the most common audience for speech bubbles but, depending on the purpose, other audiences can include students, teachers, parents, and the wider community. Teachers or students can create the images and fill in the bubbles.

How Speech bubbles are relatively easy to implement and do not require a lot of preparation. Although they can take multiple forms, typically they include a photograph or other representation of a person or group whose words appear in the bubble. Speech bubbles can be posted on walls, bulletin boards, sticky notes, posters, panels, student lockers, or cubbies inside or outside the classroom. They can also be laminated for reuse. Speech bubbles can be included in a classroom newsletter, attached to the contents of portfolios, or shared online or via PowerPoint. The computer program Comic Life (see figure 12) is an inexpensive and easy way for children and adults to create speech bubble collages.

Figure 12. Comic Life Documentation from Amanda Van Vleck's Classroom

149

What goes inside a speech bubble? During small- or whole-group discussions, listen for insightful or provocative questions or comments that reflect one or more of the following:

- Ideas that move thinking forward
- Misconceptions about key concepts
- Collaborative learning
- Important questions or disagreements
- Voices that are seldom heard
- Multiple responses to a single prompt

Variations and Extensions

- Attach speech bubbles to things that belong to children in the classroom such as cubbies, lockers, and folders.
- Laminate speech bubbles and use an erasable marker so you can reuse them.
- Post photographs and speech bubbles of teachers' thinking.
- Use speech bubbles for conversations or comments that you would like to share at your next parent–teacher conference.
- Give parents a blank speech bubble and ask them to fill in something surprising or provocative their child said that can be brought back to the classroom.
- Create thought bubbles along with speech bubbles to highlight the difference between thinking and speaking.
- For classrooms with learning centers, create signs using children's words.
- Ask students to write their thoughts or reflections about a particular topic on sticky notes. Put them on a wall to identify common themes or patterns.

If You Only Have Five Minutes . . .

- Keep an ear out for noteworthy comments from students or adults, jot them down, and share them at the beginning of the next class.
- Do the previous activity but write the comments directly into laminated speech bubbles.
- Ask students to engage in one or both of the previous activities.

Chapter 14
Engaging Families in Supporting Student Learning

This chapter provides resources to inform families about making learning visible more generally, their own child's learning in particular, and how to support children's learning at home. Tools range from a refrigerator reminder to guidelines for families interested in forming their own study group.

Tool 17. Introducing Families to Making Learning Visible
Here, we suggest different ways to introduce MLV ideas to families.

Tool 18. Refrigerator Reminder: Five Ways to Make Learning Visible at Home
This tool was created by a study group of parents at the Wickliffe Progressive Community School in Upper Arlington, Ohio, who spent a year investigating how to make learning visible at home. The reminder offers simple suggestions for documenting and encouraging group learning at home.

Tool 19. Making Learning Visible Family Survey
This short survey gives families different options for supporting children's learning in the classroom or at home.

Tool 20. Involving Families in the Learning Process
In this tool, we suggest different ways to involve families more actively in their children's learning. We also include a note created by teacher Melissa Tonachel that explains to families why they might not see their child's work displayed on every bulletin board.

Tool 21. Documenting Learning at Home
In this tool, we propose different ways that families can document children's learning at home.

17 INTRODUCING FAMILIES TO MAKING LEARNING VISIBLE

You can introduce families to the principles and ideas in this book by sharing examples with students' family members, looking at learning portraits or other readings, or facilitating a conversation about what learning looks like. Following are six suggestions for launching a conversation about learning in groups and documentation with families (for additional ideas visit www.makinglearningvisibleresources.org/engaging-families.html). You can share the readings or video at a back-to-school night to provide a common experience or at a family–teacher book club or a one-time event. Families who want to learn more can use the links to access the complete video and readings.

1. Watch one or more excerpts from Ben Mardell's (2006) "Learning Is a Team Sport: Kindergartners Study the Boston Marathon" video as a way to challenge adult assumptions about children's capabilities and launch a conversation with families about the value of learning in groups (http://vimeo.com/21372133).

2. Read Juriaan de Jong's (2006) reflection on a homework assignment from his daughter's kindergarten teacher to launch a discussion about supporting children's learning at home (www.makinglearningvisibleresources.org/an-elementary-school-parentrsquos-reflections.html).

   From Juriaan de Jong's reflection in chapter 9: "I have learned that through brainstorming together, putting my child in the driver's seat, documenting her thoughts and actions, and helping her to put them together as something concrete, I help her to open her mind and learn to think—and in the process I can feel my mind is more open as well—and I am having a lot more fun!"

3. Read and discuss Mara Krechevsky's (2009) essay "Why Don't You Tell the Other Kids?" about the impact of Reggio ideas on the way she interacts with children—in particular, her four-year-old son (www.makinglearningvisibleresources.org/ldquowhy-donrsquot-you-tell-the-other-kidsrdquo.html).

   From Mara Krechevsky's reflection: "Since my encounter with Reggio, I have changed the way I interact with children. I don't accept an initial 'I don't know.' I allow for silence. I wait more. I encourage children to share their ideas with other children, and refer them to other children to find things out. I try to understand and explore their world view for longer, rather than lead them (even if ever-so-gently) to another one. I value whimsy and fantasy along with science in the development of their theories."

4. Read a chapter or learning portrait in this book or a visual essay from *Making Learning Visible* (2001) or a related article (www.makinglearningvisibleresources.org/books-and-articles-list.html) and hold a discussion with parents and other family members. (Visual

essays are also downloadable at http://www.pz.gse.harvard.edu/making_learning_visible.php

5. Facilitate a conversation at an open house about the visibility of learning using questions such as "Do you think of learning as visible? Always? Sometimes? Never? Where might you focus a camera or when might you turn on a tape recorder or otherwise try to capture learning?"

6. Look closely at student work or other documentation in a whole or small group at an open house, family night, or other school gathering and facilitate a conversation using one of the protocols in tools 7 through 9 in chapter 12 or see-think-wonder described in tool 5 in chapter 11.

If You Only Have Five Minutes . . .

- Share student work at open house, family night, or other public events.
- Bring student work to family conferences.
- When you send grades or report cards home, include a quote from a child about learning.
- Hand out refrigerator reminders (tool 18) or making learning visible family surveys (tool 19).

18 REFRIGERATOR REMINDER: FIVE WAYS TO MAKE LEARNING VISIBLE AT HOME

Sometimes adults do not know how to respond to or take full advantage of the opportunity for learning when children ask them a question or show them a piece of work. Refrigerator reminders were developed by parents in a study group at the Wickliffe Progressive Community School in Upper Arlington, Ohio, as a simple way to help caregivers listen to children and support their learning at home. The reminders offer simple suggestions for what family members can say or do to encourage children to deepen and share their thinking, learn from and with others, and take greater ownership of their learning. The following example can be handed out at an open house or back-to-school night or sent home to families at the beginning of the year with a short explanation about supporting children's learning at home.

Five Ways to Make Learning Visible at Home

1. Don't answer, ask questions!
   When your child asks you a question, don't give the answer. Instead, ask, "What do you think?"

2. Encourage group learning at home!
   Ask your child(ren) to come up with answers or solutions together with siblings, friends, or classmates. You can also turn some homework into family homework and learn together.

3. Write it down!
   When your child brings home special artwork, ask him or her to tell you about it. Write down what your child says and store the documentation with the artwork. Or write a short quote from your child below the work itself and frame it all together.

4. Take pictures!
   Photograph your child playing at home, helping you cook, on a trip, or doing anything! Print the photographs and discuss them with your child. Ask questions such as "Tell me about this. How did you feel about doing this? Why did you choose to do this?" Document what your child says during the reflection time.

5. Extend the learning!
   When your child is really excited about a school project or takes an intense interest in something, take some time to research it further at the library, the museum, the park, or appropriate location.

Variations and Extensions

- Provide a space on the reminder for families to fill in their own ideas or ask them to create their own refrigerator reminders.
- Invite family members to role-play a conversation with a child.
- Put the reminders in a public place such as the front office.

19 MAKING LEARNING VISIBLE FAMILY SURVEY

Family surveys list different options for caregivers to become involved in MLV classrooms. Hand out surveys at the beginning of the year to get a sense for family interests and how they might be willing to help.

Name: _____

Best way to be contacted (e-mail, phone, etc.): _____

I would be interested in

_____ Responding to teachers' documentation of children's learning at school

_____ Helping to document children's learning in the classroom

_____ Helping to transcribe audio or video recordings of children's conversations

_____ Helping to edit and upload documentation (photos, video, text) to the web

_____ Documenting children's learning at home

_____ Participating in an adult study group about children's learning

_____ Contributing to an exhibition, class website, or newsletter about children's learning created by parents and other caregivers

_____ Becoming a point person to help plan occasional parent meetings, orient new families to documentation, and so on

_____ Other (please specify): _____

_____

Other comments, interests, or questions:

Variations and Extensions

- Create your own survey or ask interested families to create or collaborate with you on creating one.
- Distribute surveys after an informational meeting about supporting learning through documentation.
- Ask one or two caregivers, paraprofessionals, interns, or students to tabulate and summarize survey responses.

# 20 INVOLVING FAMILIES IN THE LEARNING PROCESS

Often family members are brought into the learning process as an audience at the end of a project or unit when there is a finished product or as recipients of grades or comments on a report card. Consider asking families to participate at the beginning or middle of a unit.

Invite Families into the Learning Process

Ask families to share thoughts, resources, and hopes at the beginning of a unit or invite families in during a unit to help solve a problem, provide feedback, contribute expertise to student projects, or investigate a topic with students. Other ideas include the following:

- Share a lesson, project, or unit plan with family members to solicit their ideas and identify resources they might provide before beginning the activities.
- Invite family members in midway through a unit to look closely at and respond to student work.
- Ask students to teach family members a key concept or skill such as a homework assignment.

Send Photographs or Cameras Home

For some learners, pictures or video will elicit more language than written notes. Try sending photographs or others images of learning home instead of or along with notes. You can also send home inexpensive digital cameras so children can share photos or video with their families and then bring the cameras back to school. Ask families to donate digital cameras they no longer use to the classroom.

Create Learning Tours with Bulletin Boards

Bulletin boards offer another way to involve families in the learning. Invite children to give families a learning tour of the bulletin board—a structured way parents can engage in the documentation of children's learning. You can also pose questions on the bulletin board with sticky notes for viewer responses.

If you do not include every child's work in your displays, caregivers may wonder or express concern about why their child's work is missing. "Another Way to Think about Bulletin Boards" is a note created by Melissa Tonachel, a kindergarten–first grade teacher, to introduce families to another way to make children's learning visible. The note encourages families to consider how individual learning can be reflected in the group and vice versa. We encourage you to adapt this note for your own setting.

Variations and Extensions

- Create your own bulletin board note.
- Ask the learners to create a bulletin board note.
- Include a note in your newsletter, e-mails to parents, blog, or letters.

Another Way to Think about Bulletin Boards

by Melissa Tonachel

When we think of classroom bulletin boards we often hold an image of a wall of similar pictures, one for each child in the class. We get a glimpse of one assignment and how each child responded to it. We hope to do something different in this space, and in so doing we are taking a risk that you will enter into a new consideration of our classroom work.

This space outside our classroom provides a window into the learning happening inside our classroom. It is not meant to offer evidence about how any particular child is succeeding. Rather, you might imagine here that you are looking through the wall into our classroom, where small groups of children are engaged in pursuing a variety of problems in different ways. All of the children in kindergarten are exploring materials and processes that lead them to new discoveries and questions. Our hope is that the documentation here allows you to appreciate the activity of learning (beyond the specific activities themselves).

Where Is My Child's Work?

Although you might not see a product of each child in the class, the experience of every child is represented here. Children participate in different ways at different moments. While three children are showing their work during a work share meeting, many others are responding to it—and as they do so, they stretch their own thinking, provide their own ideas, ask questions of themselves, and make plans for how they might approach a task next.

Who Decides?

Teachers usually decide what is wall-worthy. We often hang students' "best work" or the results of a critical assignment. What we hang on our bulletin boards, after all, is a reflection not only of the children but of ourselves as teachers: we reveal our values, our aesthetic, our pedagogy, and philosophy. We also care very much that our students' efforts are appreciated and we hope that passersby will stop and look.

This space is defined by the students. We have talked about how this wall gives people who don't usually come inside our classroom a chance to see what work we are doing. When the children were asked recently to consider the work they'd been doing and

(Continued)

---

which work they thought most important to share with people outside our classroom, they immediately identified the work you now see here. Not only did they choose the kind of work to show you, they made suggestions for how it might be displayed so that you might best appreciate it.

You, Too

The children, too, hope that you will stop and look. Beyond that, you might add your questions, ideas, and impressions. In this way, you will be participating in the work share; your voice will be brought back to the children so that when they consider each other's perspectives, they will consider yours as well. You will have a hand in moving their learning forward.

Thank you for taking the time to look carefully at our work.

21 DOCUMENTING LEARNING AT HOME

With a little support, families can document learning at home. Try facilitating tool 8 in chapter 12 with families first in order to give them a common experience of collecting and analyzing documentation. You can also do this activity with parents and teachers together. Let parents know that although some children may be self-conscious at first, over time they will become more comfortable. If children ask to see their image, you might respond, "I'm not going to show you now because I want you to focus on what you're doing."

Guidelines for Documenting Learning at Home

- Choose a focus question for your documentation related to some aspect of learning (e.g., playing or studying with peers, preparing an oral report, practicing an instrument). Try to capture different moments of the learning process.
- Identify what tools (camera, pencil and paper, smartphone, etc.) will be most useful for collecting the documentation. Keep in mind that photos are especially effective for capturing the emotional aspects of learning.
- If possible, collect two kinds of documentation (e.g., photographs plus quotes).
- Select some of the documentation you collect (e.g., a short series of photographs, a few minutes of video, etc.) to review with others. Try using one of the protocols or thinking routines in this book to structure the conversation (see tool 5 in chapter 11 or tools 7 through 9 in chapter 12).
- Share what you learned with the learners. Consider making the documentation visible (in the kitchen or hall, in a family album, on Facebook, on a laptop or DVD, etc.).

Variations and Extensions

- Encourage families to ask questions that get children to reflect on their learning.
- Ask families to respond to documentation sent home from school.
- Invite interested families to form a family or teacher–family study group to investigate a shared question about learning. Study group guidelines include the following:
  - Designate one or two facilitators.
  - Choose a question that addresses some aspect of learning.
  - Collect, view, and discuss documentation related to your question at regular intervals.
  - Use protocols or thinking routines to structure conversations.
  - Share what you learn with others.

Chapter 15
Making Learning Visible beyond the Classroom

This chapter provides tools and templates for creating bulletin boards, exhibit panels, and schoolwide exhibitions that make learning and learners visible in the school and larger community.

Tool 22. Bulletin Boards That Make Learning and Learners Visible
Here, we provide guidelines for creating bulletin boards that go beyond the typical display to make learning visible inside and outside the classroom.

Tool 23. Creating Exhibitions of Teaching and Learning
Exhibitions can serve multiple purposes and audiences. In this tool, we offer guidelines for creating an exhibition of teaching and learning for the general public. (Visit www.makinglearningvisibleresources.org/creating-an-exhibition-of-teaching-and-learning.html to see a sample exhibition brochure from Cambridge Rindge and Latin School in Cambridge, Massachusetts.)

Tool 24. Anatomy of an Exhibit Panel
This tool identifies key components to consider, such as title, context, supporting artifacts, analysis or interpretation, and format, when making learning visible beyond the classroom.

Tool 25. Zoom Guidelines and Template
In this tool, developed by Ben Mardell and his colleagues at the Eliot-Pearson Children's School at Tufts University, we provide guidelines and a template for one type of exhibit panel called Zooms. Zooms are 3' × 4' documentation panels that provide a close look at and analysis of one or more aspects of classroom life.

22 BULLETIN BOARDS THAT MAKE LEARNING AND LEARNERS VISIBLE

Bulletin boards serve multiple purposes. They convey a variety of information from meeting announcements and parent news to curriculum overviews and displays of student work. When bulletin boards focus on what was learned as well as what was done, they also make learning and learners visible. Bulletin boards share the learning process as well as product, and balance content learning with learning about learning. Often they include what the adult learned as well as students. Bulletin boards that make learning and learners visible accomplish the following:

- Communicate and promote values about teaching and learning
- Reflect a class's, or school's identity
- Make individual thinking available to the group
- Support collective knowledge building and reflection
- Help learners make connections across units and subject matter

Who Bulletin boards have many potential audiences: students, teachers, parents, administrators, and the wider community. If possible, find a colleague with whom to work in putting your board together. You can also involve students in what goes on the board by doing the following:

- Ask them what part of their learning they most want to share with others and what they most want to know from viewers; specific questions elicit the most useful feedback.
- Include students' reflections on their learning: what was hard, surprising, or exciting?
- Work with students to put the board together and reflect on it once it is done.

How Bulletin boards span the range from simple to complex and can be created during or after a learning experience. Sometimes it is more powerful to document the experience of one small group or learning moment than an entire class or unit. Beware of including too much text. If you are feeling overwhelmed, ask yourself, "What is the learning I want to make visible?" Put your name, the age or grade of the students, and date on the board (ideally in the same place on every board).

Making learning visible inside and outside the classroom are very different endeavors. Creating a board outside the classroom requires sufficient context for viewers to make sense of the board's contents; it enables a dialogue and comparison of ideas, beliefs, and values about learning and teaching. Following are considerations to guide your choices about what to include on your bulletin board:

- What is the learning that excites you the most? What are your students excited about?
- Identify your audience(s) and your goal in making the board.
- Make sure your commentary or interpretation is supported by the documentation on the board.
- What else might you include that would promote additional learning?

Bulletin Board Checklist

Did you . . .

- Include a brief context?
- Include students' work, words, and photos?
- Create an engaging title (possibly phrased as a question or a quote from a student)?
- Enlarge or otherwise highlight the phrases you consider most important?
- Solicit commentary from viewers?

Variations and Extensions

- Test out the board on others to make sure it is clear and understandable.
- Make time to revisit and reflect on the bulletin board with learners.
- Create a bulletin board about works in progress.
- Put speech bubbles on a bulletin board.
- Ask students to gather information, take pictures, or jot down quotes for the board.
- Take a learning walk around the school with colleagues or students to see what learning is visible and what the walls communicate about the identity of the school. Ask students to give their parents a bulletin board tour.
- Pair up with another classroom to read and respond to each other's bulletin boards over time.
- Post an explanatory note to viewers sharing your bulletin board philosophy.
- Think broadly: bulletin boards can be inside or outside the classroom, physical or virtual (e.g., blogs, wikis, or newsletters).

If You Only Have Five Minutes . . .

- Add pictures if you typically put up only text, or text if you typically put up only pictures.
- Add your own reflection on learning to the board.
- Add a photograph or two about the learning process to the board.
- Add one layer at a time to a bulletin board; for example, student reflections, the learning context, an engaging title, teacher reflections, the learning process, or an invitation for public commentary.

23 CREATING EXHIBITIONS OF TEACHING AND LEARNING

Most of the information the public receives about student learning takes the form of test scores or dispiriting news stories. Exhibitions of teaching and learning offer another way to make learning public. Exhibitions can serve multiple purposes and audiences: they can hold teachers and students accountable to each other and the community and they can serve as a political act to provoke assumptions, values, and beliefs about teaching and learning and the role of school in society.

Creating and reflecting on exhibits is a powerful form of professional development that deepens the exhibitors' learning through the hard but rewarding work of communicating student and adult learning. Exhibitions of teaching and learning can do the following:

- Share and celebrate student and teacher learning
- Challenge unexamined notions of students' capabilities and provoke conversation about teaching and learning in the wider community
- Provide a form of self-assessment related to the school's mission
- Offer evidence of the kinds of learning not often reflected in standardized tests
- Contribute to our collective knowledge about how children learn

Who Exhibitions can be created by and shared with multiple audiences including teachers, students, families, administrators, the school board, and the wider community. Identifying one or two point people to oversee the creation process is critical, with an advisory committee to help with decision making and details. Exhibit panels (or video) can be created by individuals or teams. Depending on the goals of the exhibition, students can be consulted about what part of their learning they most want to share and what they most want to learn from viewers. Students can also contribute to creating an exhibit and reflecting on the finished product.

How Perhaps the most distinctive feature of exhibitions is that they focus on learning, not just what was done. Exhibitions can focus on teachers or students, the learning process or product, learning content or learning about learning, or all of the above! They can be designed to address a schoolwide or exhibition-specific topic (e.g., the role of questioning in learning) or have diverse foci. Exhibit panels usually tell targeted stories of learning (e.g., of a small group or powerful learning moment) that enable creators and viewers to go deeper rather than cover an entire project or unit. They can expand on astonishing or unusual moments of learning or moments when learning gets stuck. Because exhibitions will likely represent a new venue for parent–teacher interactions, send a letter in advance or include a note in the brochure about the difference between an exhibition and family–teacher conference that is focused on one's own child.

Typical components of exhibit panels include photographs, text, students' work and reflections, and adult analysis (see tool 24). Supporting material should be positioned near the related text to make the connection clear for viewers. Exhibits communicate most effectively when there is a shared esthetic with regard to layout, ratio of pictures to text, graphics (use of mounting, font style, and size), color, text structure and flow, and balance of child and adult voices. Always beware of including too much text.

Exhibitions can be held in the middle or end of the year in a school auditorium, library, hall, or individual classrooms. They can also be held in other public arenas such as the town library, community center, or city hall. Useful thinking routines for reflecting on exhibits include see-think-wonder (see tool 5 in chapter 11) and connect-extend-challenge (see www.visiblethinkingpz.org).

The following is one possible scenario for opening night and subsequent activities:

- Begin with structured remarks by two or more of the following: administrator, teacher, parent, politician, and student.
- Allow time for roaming. Ask viewers to post or leave reflections on sticky notes.
- Set aside time to facilitate structured conversations around one or more exhibits using a simple protocol.
- Designate other public viewing times.
- Choose pairs of exhibits to rotate through public places during the year. Offer a series of brown bag lunches that focus on one or two exhibits at a time.
- Use a staff meeting for teachers to view and reflect on each other's exhibits.
- Document or archive the exhibits. Share them with new teachers or families.

Variations and Extensions

- Test exhibits on others to make sure they communicate effectively.
- Create a studio or workshop type of exhibition to solicit feedback on works in progress.
- Focus on one grade level or subject matter at a time.
- Invite designated respondents to post responses to the exhibits.
- Ask students to help document, take pictures, add reflections, or create their own exhibit.
- Post exhibits on your school website.
- Host a panel discussion related to the exhibits.
- Create a museum of learning with rotating exhibits throughout the year.

24 ANATOMY OF AN EXHIBIT PANEL

Documentation serves many purposes. Some documentation supports learners inside the learning group; other documentation is directed toward those outside the learning group. This tool describes five key features of exhibit panels or documentation boards that are shared beyond the learning group.

Who This tool is useful for teachers, administrators, students, and others interested in sharing documentation for public viewing.

How Consider the components listed in this tool when creating a documentation board or exhibit panel for display. (Also, see tool 25 for a template and guidelines related to one type of exhibit panel called Zooms that depicts snapshots of classroom life).

As with the other tools in this section, remember the following:

- Beware of including too much written text.
- Try to balance metacognitive learning and learning content.
- Documenting the experience of one small group, moment, or event is often more powerful than documenting an entire lesson or unit.
- If you are feeling adrift in a sea of data, ask yourself, "What is the learning I want to make visible?"

Title
A good title gives the viewer an immediate sense for your piece and the intended meaning of the panel. Consider using a quote, metaphor, or anything else that will pique viewer interest and convey what the learning is about. The title should be prominently placed and large enough to draw the viewer's attention.

Context
Try to limit the context to one or two short paragraphs of background information that will set the stage for viewers. The context should include the teacher or documenter name(s), the age group of the learners, the names of the school and town, the purpose of the learning experience, and the date or time period. Put photos or images of the learners up front. Other information you might include is the learning prompt or project, the size of the group, related previous experiences, and materials used. Photographs or other images can be efficient ways to provide some of this information.

Supporting Artifacts

Carefully choose from the various artifacts you collect, such as transcripts, photographs, student work, and the like. Pick the documents that are most critical for helping viewers see how you came to your interpretations about learning (see following) and also allow for other interpretations. The artifacts should represent the learning process as well as the product—the how as well as the what of learning. If possible, choose at least two media, for example, text (narrative or quotes) and images, to display.

Your Analysis or Interpretation

Include your own learning in the panel. What excited or surprised you about the experience of the learners? What furthered your own thinking? What connections can you make to broader issues or images of teaching and learning? Consider including brief reflections throughout the piece to communicate your interpretation of the documentation. What story of learning do you want to tell? What conversations would you like to provoke? How will the documentation help you shape future learning experiences?

Format

Decide on a uniform format for your documentation boards and exhibit panels so viewers won't have to figure out how to read them every time you post something. Try formatting your documentation on a computer or by hand on standard-sized paper (8.5" × 11" or 14") rather than big posters. This allows the documentation to be easily copied and distributed to colleagues for feedback or added to over time. If you put up panels, their size will depend on the setting. Dimensions of 3' × 4' are often manageable. Viewers should be able to take in the key information in roughly five to ten minutes. For those interested in exploring the work more deeply, you can provide additional information or artifacts on a table or nearby wall.

25 ZOOM GUIDELINES AND TEMPLATE

It is often hard to know where to start or how to organize your data when creating an exhibit panel that makes your own or your students' learning visible. Zooms are 3' × 4' documentation panels that provide an effective and efficient way to communicate teacher and student learning. They include photographs, conversation snippets, children's work, and adult reflection or analysis. Zooms offer a close look at children's and teachers' responses to or understandings of a question related to teaching and learning. Zooms were initially developed in 2009 by Ben Mardell and his colleagues at the Eliot-Pearson Children's School in Medford, Massachusetts (www.naeyc.org/files/naeyc/file/Voices_Zooms.pdf). The Zoom guidelines and template provide a useful format for teachers engaged in schoolwide inquiry.

How Use the guidelines and template on the following pages to design your own zoom. See tool 24 for a more general discussion of the components of exhibit panels.

Zoom Panel Guidelines and Template

Layout
To help the readability of your panel,

- The text or other information should be read from left to right.

- Consider numbering the panel sections to signal "read this first," "read this second," and so on.

- Ask a colleague for feedback regarding the clarity of your layout.

- Consider using a consistent typeface at a minimum 36 points for titles, 20 points for other text.

- Make the points or phrases you consider most important stand out.

Title
A good title gives viewers an immediate sense for your piece and addresses a central aspect of the intended meaning of the documentation. Consider using a metaphor or

(Continued)

---

student's words—anything that will pique viewer interest and convey what the learning is about. The title should be prominently placed in the top left.

Question

The question addressed in your panel should be connected to supporting individual and group learning and your own or your school's educational values and interests. Ideally, a good question should also do the following:

- Be of interest and value to other educators.

- Relate to a topic students could help you investigate.

- Be a manageable size (e.g., grounded in something you already do in the classroom).

- Be aesthetically pleasing to you and others (e.g., succinct, inspiring).

See tool 12 in chapter 13 for examples of guidelines to create questions. For example, "How can sixth-graders become better listeners?" or "What happens when children contribute to choosing small groups?" or "When is a piece of work finished?" Be prepared to revise your question several times before settling on a final version.

Context

Try to keep the context to no more than two short paragraphs of background information that set the stage for viewers. The context should include the who, what, where, when, and why of the panel (teacher-documenter name[s], age group of learners, name of school and town, date or time period described, purpose of the learning experience, and what motivated your question). Place photos or images of learners in the upper left-hand corner. The context can also include the learning prompt or project, size of the group, related previous experiences, or materials used.

Zoom-in (Moments of Learning)

From the artifacts you collect (transcripts, photographs, student work, etc.), carefully select the documents that are most critical for enabling viewers to see how you arrived at your interpretations about learning (see following). Try to include something about the learning process (the how) as well as the product (the what).

Zoom-out (Findings or Analysis and Implications)

This section describes what you learned. It includes two parts that can be combined into one: the meaning you make of the zoom-in moment (findings or analysis) and your sense of the larger implications for teaching and learning more generally (implications). Include brief reflections throughout the context and zoom-in sections as well. What story of learning do you want to tell? What was exciting or surprising to you about the learners' experience? What furthered your own thinking? How will the documentation help you shape future learning? What connections can you make to broader issues of teaching and learning?

Compelling **Title** (Should be large/bold enough to draw the eye here first. Either position at the top left OR, if centered, help the viewer navigate from the title to where they should look next.)

Zoom Out

Findings/Analysis

Implications

Teacher(s)
Classroom
Date

Zoom In

You can include a short visual essay or other artifacts from the learning experience that provide a closer look at moments or work that relate to your question and the learning you want to show.

Captions should be included with any images that need an explanation.

Question

Context

Figure 13. Zoom Template

About the Authors

Mara Krechevsky is a senior researcher at Project Zero at the Harvard Graduate School of Education. She is the research director of the Making Learning Visible (MLV) project, an investigation into documenting and assessing individual and group learning in US classrooms. MLV is based on collaborative research with educators from the municipal preschools of Reggio Emilia, Italy. Mara was also the director of Project Spectrum, a ten-year research project implementing multiple intelligences theory in early childhood. She has written numerous articles and provided professional development for hundreds of teachers and administrators in the United States and abroad on the theory of multiple intelligences and the pedagogy of Reggio Emilia and their implications for education. Mara is the author of *Project Spectrum: Preschool Assessment Handbook*, a coauthor of *Making Learning Visible: Children as Individual and Group Learners* and *Making Teaching Visible: Documenting Individual and Group Learning as Professional Development*, and a general editor of the three-volume series *Project Zero Frameworks for Early Childhood Education*. Mara is also a resident limericist at Project Zero.

Ben Mardell is an associate professor in early childhood education at Lesley University and a researcher on the Making Learning Visible project at Project Zero at the Harvard Graduate School of Education. For the past twenty-five years, Ben has taught and conducted research with infants, toddlers, preschoolers, and kindergartners. He is the author of *From Basketball to the Beatles: In Search of Compelling Early Childhood Curriculum* and *Growing Up in Child Care: A Case for Quality Early Education,* and a coauthor of *Making Learning Visible: Children as Individual and Group Learners* and *Making Teaching Visible: Documentation of Individual and Group Learning as Professional Development*. Recently, Ben has begun competing in sprint triathlons.

Melissa Rivard is a researcher and visual media specialist for the Making Learning Visible and World in Portland projects at Project Zero. She has collaborated with hundreds of teachers and administrators, domestically and abroad, exploring ways to make learning and teaching a more visible, collaborative, and democratic process. Melissa helped to establish the Documentation Studio at Wheelock College—the first venue in the United States dedicated to the study and practice of documentation as a pedagogical tool for preschool to postsecondary educators. She has mounted more than a dozen exhibitions of teacher and student learning and produced numerous videos that serve as professional development for teachers and provide windows into learning for the larger public. Recent films include *Documentation: Transforming Our Perspective* (based on interviews with key educators and scholars in Reggio Emilia, Italy) and *The Color Investigation: Making Learning Visible in a K0–K1 Classroom*. She is the coauthor of several journal articles and coeditor and producer of the book and DVD set *The Ohio Visible Learning Project: Stories from Wickliffe Progressive Community School*. Melissa enjoys foraging for mushrooms and tending her rooftop garden.

Daniel G. Wilson is a principal investigator at Harvard Graduate School of Education's Project Zero, where he has collaborated not only on the Making Children Visible project on which this book is based but also on the YMCA Early Learning project and the Learning Innovations Laboratories project. He is particularly interested in professional learning communities, group learning, and team performance. Daniel publishes and speaks worldwide. Since 1995, he has given keynote addresses in such diverse places as Mexico, Colombia, and Sweden. In 2010, he delivered workshops and seminars in Ecuador, Colombia, and New York City. Music is one of his lifelong passions, and he plays drums and percussion in two Boston-based bands.

Notes

Foreword

1. Vygotsky, L. S. (1978). *Mind in society: The development of higher psychological processes.* Cambridge, MA: Harvard University Press.

Introduction

1. Edwards, C., Gandini, L., and Forman, G. (Eds.). (2012). *The hundred languages of children: The Reggio Emilia experience in transformation* (p. 58). Santa Barbara, CA: Praeger.
2. Ibid., p. 57.

Chapter 7: Making Learning and Learners Visible

1. For more information on these books and the different phases of the Making Learning Visible research, see www.mlvpz.org
2. Partnership for 21st Century Skills. (2002). *Learning for the 21st century.* Washington, DC: Author.
3. For more details of this performance view of understanding, see Perkins, D. (1998). What is understanding? In M. S. Wiske (Ed.), *Teaching for understanding: Linking research with practice.* San Francisco: Jossey-Bass.
4. Perkins, D. (2008). *Making learning whole: How seven principles of teaching can transform education.* San Francisco: Jossey-Bass.
5. Sizer, T. (1992). *Horace's school: Redesigning the American high school.* Boston: Houghton Mifflin.
6. Wiske, M. S. (Ed.). (1998). *Teaching for understanding: Linking research with practice.* San Francisco: Jossey-Bass.
7. Vygotsky, L. S. (1978). *Mind in society.* Cambridge, MA: Harvard University Press.
8. Bandura, A. (1977). *Social learning theory.* New York: General Learning Press.
9. Deci, E. L., and Flaste, R. (1996). *Why we do what we do: Understanding self-motivation.* New York: Penguin.
10. Csikszentmihalyi, M., Rathunde, K., and Whalen, S. (1993). *Talented teenagers: The roots of success and failure.* Cambridge, UK: Cambridge University Press.
11. Damasio, A. (2000). *The feeling of what happens: Body and emotion in the making of consciousness.* New York: Harcourt Brace.
12. Knowles, M. (1975). *Self-directed learning: A guide for learners and teachers.* New York: Association Press.
13. Partnership for 21st Century Skills. (2002). *Learning for the 21st century.* Washington, DC: Author.
14. Gardner, H. (1983). *Frames of mind: The theory of multiple intelligences.* New York: Basic Books.
15. Process folios contain a history of the student's learning process, tracing the biography of samples of student work from start to finish. See Gardner, H. (1989). Project Zero: An introduction to arts propel. *Journal of Art & Design Education, 8,* 167–182.

Chapter 8: Unpacking the Practice of Group Learning

1. Krechevsky, M., and Mardell, B. (2001). Four features of learning in groups. In Project Zero and Reggio Children, *Making learning visible: Children as individual and group learners*. Reggio Emilia, Italy: Reggio Children.

2. Vygotsky, L. (1978). *Mind in society: The development of higher psychological processes*. Cambridge, MA: Harvard University Press.

3. See, for example, Johnson, D. W., and Johnson, R. T. (1995). *Learning together and alone: Cooperative, competitive and individualistic learning* (4th ed.). Boston: Allyn & Bacon; Slavin, R. (1995). *Cooperative learning: Theory, research and practice* (2nd ed.). Boston: Allyn & Bacon.

4. Seidel, S. (2001). To be part of something bigger than oneself. In Project Zero and Reggio Children, *Making learning visible: Children as individual and group learners*. Reggio Emilia, Italy: Reggio Children.

5. http://www.pz.gse.harvard.edu/making_learning_visible.php

6. Webb, N., Farivar, S., and Matergeorge, A. (2002). Productive helping in cooperative groups. *Theory Into Practice, 41*(1), 13–20.

7. Lindy had learned about these questions from reading about the work of fifth-sixth grade teacher Sarah Fiarman in Mardell, B., Turner, T., Bucco, C., Donovan, M., Fiarman, S., Hamel, I., Krechevsky, M., Monahan, D., Seidel, S., Sutter, C., and Thies, A. (2003). *Making teaching visible: Documentation of individual and group learning as professional development*. Cambridge, MA: Project Zero.

8. Lotan, R. (2003). Group-worthy tasks. *Educational Leadership, 6*, 72–75.

9. Hawkins, D. (2012). Malaguzzi's story, other stories and respect for children. In C. Edwards, L. Gandini, and G. Forman (Eds.), *The hundred languages of children: The Reggio Emilia experience in transformation*. Santa Barbara, CA: Praeger.

10. Alexander, R. (2008). *Towards dialogic teaching* (4th ed.). York, England: Dialogos.

11. Michaels, S., O'Connor, M. C., Hall, M. W., and Resnick, L. (2010). *Accountable Talk® sourcebook: For classroom conversation that works*. Pittsburgh: Institute for Learning.

12. McDonald, J., Mohr, N., Dichter, A., and McDonald, E. (2003). *The power of protocols: An educator's guide to better practice*. New York: Teachers College Press.

13. Ritchhart, R., Church, M., and Morrison, K. (2011). *Making thinking visible: How to promote engagement, understanding, and independence for all learners*. San Francisco: Jossey-Bass.

14. Andrade, H. G. (2000). Using rubrics to promote thinking and learning. *Educational Leadership, 57*(5), 13–18.

15. Berger, R. (2003). *An ethic of excellence: Building a culture of craftsmanship with students*. Portsmouth, NH: Heinemann.

16. Mardell, B. (2012). Making learning visible at the Lee Academy pilot school. In G. Perry (Ed.), *Our inquiry, our practice: Undertaking, supporting and learning from teacher research(ers)*. Washington, DC: National Association for the Education of Young Children.

17. Pianta, R., Belsky, J., Houts, R., and Morrison, F. (2007). Opportunities to learn in America's elementary classrooms. *Science, 315*, 1795–1796.

18. Cohen, E. (1994). Restructuring the classroom: Conditions for productive small groups. *Review of Educational Research, 64*(1), 1–35.

19. Baker, A. (2013, January 12). Gifted, talented and separated: In one school, students are divided by gifted label—and race. New York Times. www.nytimes.com/2013/01/13/education/in-one-school-students-are-divided-by-gifted-label-and-race.html?emc=tnt&tntemail1=y

20. Project Zero and Reggio Children. (2001). *Making learning visible: Children as individual and group learners*. Reggio Emilia, Italy: Reggio Children.

21. Sutton, R., and Hargadon, A. (1996). Brainstorming in context: Effectiveness in a product design firm. *Administrative Science Quarterly, 41*(4), 685–718.

Chapter 9: Unpacking the Practice of Documentation

1. Mardell, B., Turner, T., Bucco, C., Donovan, M., Fiarman, S., Hamel, I., Krechevsky, M., Monahan, D., Seidel, S., Sutter, C., and Thies, A. (2003). *Making teaching visible: Documentation of individual and group learning as professional development.* Cambridge, MA: Project Zero.
2. Grossman, P., Wineburg, S., and Woolworth, S. (2001). Toward a theory of teacher community. *Teachers College Record, 103,* 942–1012.
3. Langer, E. (1989). *Mindfulness.* Reading, MA: Addison-Wesley.
4. Massachusetts Curriculum Framework for English Language Arts & Literacy (p. 17): ". . . students actively seek to understand other perspectives and cultures through reading and listening, and they are able to communicate effectively with people of varied backgrounds. They evaluate other points of view critically and constructively"; (p. 18): "*Speaking and listening: Flexible communication and collaboration* (students must learn to work together, express and listen carefully to ideas, integrate information from oral, visual, quantitative, and media sources, evaluate what they hear . . ."
5. Kegan, R. (1989). *The evolving self.* Cambridge, MA: Harvard University Press.
6. Forman, G., and Fyfe, B. (1998). Negotiated learning through design, documentation, and discourse. In C. Edwards, L. Gandini, and G. Forman (Eds.), *The hundred languages of children: The Reggio Emilia approach—Advanced reflections* (pp. 245–246). Greenwich, CT: Ablex.
7. To view the learning portrait, Making every voice heard, visit the MLV website: http://www.pz .gse.harvard.edu/making_learning_visible.php
8. Krechevsky, M., Rivard, M., and Burton, F. (2010). Accountability in three realms: Making learning visible inside and outside the classroom. *Theory Into Practice, 49*(1), 64–71.
9. The Documentation Studio at Wheelock College was founded in 2008 by Stephanie Cox Suarez for educators pre-K through postsecondary to share and learn from documentation together. To learn more, visit www.Wheelock.edu/DocStudio

Chapter 10: Making Learning Visible in an Age of Accountability

1. See the Common Core State Standards Initiative at http://www.corestandards.org/the-standards
2. Massachusetts Department of Education. (2006). Massachusetts science and technology/ engineering framework. www.doe.mass.edu/frameworks/scitech/1006.pdf; Massachusetts Department of Elementary and Secondary Education. (2011). Massachusetts curriculum framework for English language arts and literacy. www.doe.mass.edu/frameworks/ela/0311.pdf
3. Vecchi, V. (1996). Birth of two horses. In *Municipality of Reggio Emilia: The hundred languages of children catalog.* Reggio Emilia, Italy: Reggio Children.
4. Campbell, D. (1976). *Assessing the impact of planned social change.* Hanover, NH: The Public Affairs Center, Dartmouth College.
5. Nichols, S. L., and Berliner, D. C. (2007). *Collateral damage: How high-stakes testing corrupts America's schools.* Cambridge, MA: Harvard Education Press. Also see Darling-Hammond, L. (2009). *The flat world and education: How America's commitment to equity will determine our future.* New York: Teachers College Press.
6. See Krechevsky, M., Rivard, M., and Burton, F. (2010). Accountability in three realms: Making learning visible inside and outside the classroom. *Theory Into Practice, 49*(1), 64–71, for a fuller discussion of this view of accountability.

7. Seidel, S. (2008). Foreword: Lessons from Reggio. In L. Gandini, S. Etheredge, and L. Hill (Eds.), *Insights and inspirations from Reggio Emilia: Stories of teachers and children from North America* (pp. 14–15). Worcester, MA: Davis.

8. Krechevsky, M., Rivard, M., and Burton, F. (2010). Accountability in three realms: Making learning visible inside and outside the classroom. *Theory Into Practice, 49*(1), 64–71.

9. Vygotsky, L. (1978). *Mind in society: The development of higher psychological processes.* Cambridge, MA: Harvard University Press.

Chapter 11: Supporting Learning in Groups in the Classroom

1. Project Zero and Reggio Children. (2001). *Making learning visible: Children as individual and group learners.* Reggio Emilia, Italy: Reggio Children.

2. Aronson, E., and Patnoe, S. (2011). *Cooperation in the classroom: The jigsaw method* (3rd ed.). London: Pinter & Martin.

Chapter 13: Documenting Individual and Group Learning

1. Adapted from the protocol of the same name in Allen, D., and Blythe, T. (2003) *The facilitator's book of questions: Tools for looking together at student and teacher work.* New York: Teachers College Press.

Index

Photo Credits

All images in the book by Melissa Rivard except:

Pg. xiv (Figure 1), © Reggio Children
Pg. 13–18, Mandy Locke and Matt Leaf
Pg. 20, Joan Soble
Pg. 23 (Fever Chart), Joan Soble
Pg. 26–27, Doug McGlathery
Pg. 32, Doug McGlathery
Pg. 35–37, Ben Mardell
Pg. 39–40, 42–47, Amanda Van Vleck
Pg. 88 (Figure 5), Jennifer Hogue
Pg. 149 (Figure 12), Amanda Van Vleck